MY GARDEN AND I

MY
GARDEN
AND
I

Olive Pitkin

LYONS & BURFORD

Publishers

Interior design by Liz Driesbach
Line drawings by Karen Jacobsen

Printed in the United States of America
10 9 8 7 6 5 4 3 2 1

Library of Congress Cataloging-in Publication Data

Pitkin, Olive.
   My garden and I / Olive Pitkin.
      p.   cm.
   ISBN 1-55821-180-2
   1. Woodwinds Garden (Watch Hill, R.I.)
   2. Pitkin, Olive—Homes and haunts—
   Rhode Island—Watch Hill.   3. Gardening—Rhode
   Island—Watch Hill.   I. Title.
   SB466.U7W666   1992
   635.9'09745'9—dc20   92-24857
                                              CIP

for Igor

Contents

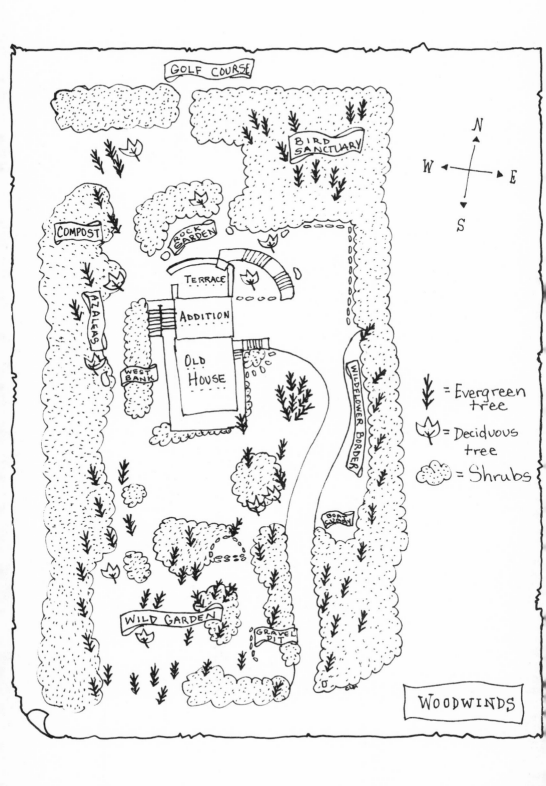

Introduction

A word of caution before you plunge in: If, when you think of a garden, you visualize prizewinning delphiniums and trimmed hedges, this book is not for you. But if your imagination, like mine, shows you the Garden of Eden in the first flush of its creation, before Adam started in with his hoe—and if you can even allow the serpent his place in the picture—then read on. That is the kind of garden this book is about (at least in principle).

Most of the people who visit me here are probably not aware that I consider myself to have a garden at all. They don't say, "Oh, I want to go out and see your garden!" or "Your garden is gorgeous!" What they do say, often, is "It's nice here" or "I like your place—there's always something to see." These mild accolades warm my heart and make me feel I have done, at least to some degree, what I set out to do: to help my little piece of ground show itself to best advantage; to heighten and enrich, but never to violate, its own essential character. I have done this by applying gardening principles and techniques, and it seems to me reasonable to call the result a garden. If you agree, we are all right so far.

What I have written here is a personal chronicle, describing how I happened to come (rather late in life) into the gardening world and how I have, over a long period of time, with much joy and a great deal of error, found my place in a small quiet corner of it. It's not a book about How To Do It Right; it's more on the order of How I Did It—And What Happened Then. Sprinkled through this account, nevertheless, you will find some collections of opinionated garden lore—ways of doing things that my garden and I have worked out over the years. Some of these methods are traditional and some, I think, are original; they may or may not work for you, but I came by them the hard way and thought they were worth sharing. It is my hope, of course, that new gardeners at least will receive these pearls with the kind of solemn and believing attention that I used to give, once upon a time, to any and all books on this noble subject. For gardeners of more experience (who have by now their own ideas), such credulousness is too much to ask; but they may find some amusement in my misadventures, and a few may even acknowledge—deep in their hearts—that it has not been so very different for them.

Woodwinds
Watch Hill, Rhode Island
February, 1992

How It Started

It was 1969, the year of the first Moon Walk, when we bought six-tenths of an acre of scrubby hillside overlooking Block Island Sound and built a small many-windowed house on it. The house had two stories and four bedrooms—just enough to accommodate my husband, myself, and our three children, then aged twelve, fourteen, and fifteen.

Up to that time we had lived and worked in New York City, spending a month each summer in a rented cottage. More and more often we had drifted toward southeastern Connecticut and the southern Rhode Island coast, especially the tiny town of Watch Hill, which thrives in the summer with yachters, golfers, and tennis players but disappears from sight in the winter. Finally, it became appropriate and feasible to have a place of our own, and when a lot became available in Watch Hill we joined the ranks of the second-homers.

The property lay in an area that was, at that time, pretty much undeveloped, though it abutted at its northern end on the rolling slopes of the Misquamicut Golf Club. From north to south it ran quite steeply downhill, ending in an absolute gully beside the dirt road that was the "front" property line. It was almost totally covered with a thicket of typical Rhode Island bush: several largish stands of red cedar, ditto of bayberry and wild blueberry of three different heights (which I have never identified as other than high, regular, and low), also some sumac, wild grapevines, and a truly astonishing amount of poison ivy. There were a number of wild cherry trees of varying ages to which I instantly lost my heart because to me they looked so much like apple trees (nobody told me they were "weeds" and unworthy of notice), and several shadbushes. It was late autumn when we bought the land, and not a flower was to be seen; I did recognize some dried-up goldenrod here and there.

Although I was happy with the idea of having a summer place of our own and thus avoiding the horrendous weekends of packing and unpacking that our previous vacations had entailed, I was not (I thought) in any position to take on more domestic responsibilities than I already had, which seemed to fill the leisure from my full-time work quite satisfactorily. "I'm not going to do any gardening," I said firmly.

I went further. Having grown up in Vermont, I cherished the idea of living in a little brown house deep in the woods (untouched and untended) and rambling comfortably through them gathering wildflowers in May or sitting with my back

2

against a stone reading poetry. "No lawn," I said. "Just a path from the driveway."

But my husband grew up on the Baltic coast and loves wide horizons. As soon as the house was high enough, he put a ladder on the deck and ascertained that by a bit of judicious topping of the cedars to the south we could actually have a glimpse of the ocean. Ignorant as I was then, I had nevertheless derived from somewhere the notion that to cut down a tree—any tree—amounted to sacrilege if not blasphemy; but I pleaded in vain. In time I found out that my husband's view is shared by many; for years I have been astonished at the number of other people who consider that little triangle of blue water to be the crowning glory of our outlook.

And I succumbed to the idea of a small lawn when it was pointed out that a goodish area south of the house had to be cleared anyway in order to install a leaching field for the septic tank. That area, I agreed reluctantly, might as well be seeded and mown. After all, it would be nice to have a place to play badminton and croquet, and I saw myself in a hammock on the edge of the lawn dozing through the long afternoons. (This was before my back went bad and I found out that of all human contraptions in the world a hammock is the most uncomfortable.)

The foundations were laid before the ground froze, and we came repeatedly through the winter to picnic on and gloat over "our property" and dream impossible dreams. Then in the spring the house went up, with a deck running around three sides of it, and on our seventeenth wedding anniversary we moved in our little bits of second-hand furniture and were at home. We called the place Woodwinds. My husband and the children played tennis and sailed and enjoyed the beach, and I sat on the deck and reveled in all that green to look at after so many years of concrete and brick.

But I have omitted one significant, symbolic, crucially indicative gesture. In the fall, even before the hole was dug for the foundation, I brought with me on one of our family picnics a dozen daffodil bulbs and with my son's help planted them among the grass near a fringe of blueberries, where we could see them from our bedroom window.

With that act—though I didn't know it then—my fate was sealed.

Enter a Non-Gardener

"I'm not going to garden," I said firmly. I never *had* gardened; I had never even seen any gardening done, to speak of. It was true that my parents had a vegetable plot in the backyard in Vermont, about twenty by thirty feet, where they raised all the vegetables our family ever ate. But they didn't believe in child labor and my only recollections of how it was done concerned a compost pile behind the garage (the nearest my mother could come to the manure pile of her farm youth) and the backbreaking toil of spading the whole area up every spring. I did remember, also, seeing my mother bring out water to her young tomato plants in July, dipping a careful pint or so around each one. This was all "gardening" meant to me and it did not appeal to me either as recreation or food supply. Those tomatoes were good, though, hot from the vine . . . and the young peas on the Fourth of July . . . But I wanted none of it. I had enough to do.

It became apparent pretty promptly, though, that we had to do *something*, here and there. You can't just sit on your deck and admire the greenery all the time; sometimes you like to move around a little and get a different view. Moving around on our property that first summer was something to be undertaken with machete in hand. The children took a shortcut to the north, across the golf course, to get to their tennis lessons, and that involved traversing a 20-foot expanse of mixed blueberries, bayberries, and roses. Not agreeable. I myself, in order to get to a stone suitable for leaning-against-with-poetry-book, had to wade through underbrush in a way that was not always convenient. Poison ivy was a constant danger, and we very soon found out that we were all "susceptible" to it.

So paths had to be cleared. I made one through that northernmost strip of scratchy scrub and two more leading up to it, one from each side of the house. I had not, at that time, read anything about the layout or design of paths (and as for the *construction* of paths, I would have thought it a contradiction in terms—and still do); but they turned out to be properly meandering because they had to go around big rocks and because it was easier to cut them through the least dense shrubbery.

Then the house looked awfully raw and square, sitting on its thin new patch of lawn. It had about a foot of exposed foundation, which didn't help. So, on our trips to the North Stonington town dump (we hadn't yet discovered the much closer local dump), which was located on a most beautiful wooded hillside, I dug up bunches of ferns and stuck them in around the house. A few wildflowers caught my eye and I stuck them in on the somewhat sunnier west side.

When I say "I stuck them in," that's just what I did. My one tool was a trowel and with it I would make a hole just big enough to hold the transplantee, shove the plant in, and push the soil back around it. Sometimes I watered them afterwards (remembering my mother's care for her tomatoes), sometimes I didn't—reasoning that because they were wild and tough they'd thrive under any abuse.

They didn't. The ferns were all right (I've since found that you can't kill a fern short of putting it in a live furnace), but the wildflowers mostly died or sat there, one by one in a straight line, looking totally pathetic and usually refusing to bloom. The ones that did bloom appeared to be doing so as an act of desperation and, having given their all, would then die. By the end of our first year these plantings could best be described as hopeless.

There was all that poison ivy to deal with. There was the raw, steep bank to the west of the house, where the space for its foundation had been gouged out of the hillside. There was that nice stretch of land sloping down to the road below the house, giving seductive intimations of woodsiness but, in its native state, altogether baffling human entry.

And finally, once I had become a bit used to the overall aspect of greenery, there was the undeniable fact that it could stand some improvement—that in fact it demanded improvement in order to be truly picturesque and usable. I had no intention of turning our country hideaway into a suburban plot, and I really *didn't* want to garden. But, I felt as I gazed and gazed, our little bit of land was not being its best self. While it was undoubtedly a diamond, it was also undoubtedly very

much in the rough. Those nice groups of bayberries, for example—they were festooned with various drooping vines and creepers and disfigured by fountains of high sea grass around their trunks. Many of the cedars had dead branches up to ten or twelve feet from the ground. As the seasons passed, I began to notice a violet here and there, and a strawberrylike ground cover with a pretty yellow flower; but these things couldn't be appreciated because they were sparse and overgrown. I was shocked to find that there wasn't a fern on the place anywhere, not a daisy, not even a buttercup. No black-eyed Susans, no Queen Anne's lace. I might not know anything about gardening, but I knew that a house in the country ought to have at least these basic field flowers. I cast my mind back to the wooded hillsides of my childhood and recalled jack-in-the-pulpit and bunchflower and trailing arbutus and lady's slipper.

Then I thought about this place as a real home, probably destined to become our retirement home and until then a place where the children could come for vacations. While we all liked the idea of a "wild place," maybe it could be tamed just a little so as to have some touches of brightness and color to mark the progress of the seasons. How about a lilac? Lilac is the very essence of home. I'd never thought about it before, but I did now. A home *should* have a lilac bush—it's just something a home should have.

I was determined to keep it a wild place, but the more I thought about it, the more my imagination conjured up a *beautiful* wild place, an ideal wild place, a twice-as-good-as-nature wild place. I began to read books about shady gardens and "natural" gardens and—looking at the glacial deposits of granite liberally strewn around—rock gardens. And I began, perforce, to learn the elements of gardening.

It's a fascinating subject, like all subjects when they are tackled seriously. I read everything and I tried—almost everything. The compost pile I had of course started immediately, with the brush cleared to open up paths. I learned about, and tried, raising plants from seed (both wild and cultivated); transplanting as it should properly be done; soil preparation and improvement; layering and other methods of propagation; pruning; garden layout and home landscaping in general. (It was a little late for that, but you have to start from where you are.)

I learned about "borrowed views." That was one thing we had plenty of: to the north the golf course and, some distance to the east, a neighbor's house, both with beautifully manicured undulations of lawn and tasteful unobtrusive plantings; to the west an apparently limitless forest of cedar and scrub, very like our own; and to the south that tantalizing glimpse of the sea over the tops of the trees. I wanted our home to be a little jewel set in the midst of all this, looking like a spontaneous condensation of the essence of the landscape. And I conceived the notion that the wildness should dissipate little by little as one came closer to the house, so that it would even be permissible to have a few real garden flowers in the area immediately surrounding the house. (This idea was checked somewhat by circumstances I will tell about later, but I still think it's a good principle and have, in a broad general way, carried it out.)

I learned about vistas, and spent hours and hours sitting here and there on the property designing them. I learned about the importance of three-dimensionality, which I think was the concept that struck me most with a shock of recognition and the excited feeling that I myself could be creative on this principle. After all, with a hillside property I had a head start on three dimensions.

I learned a great deal, and dreamed most wistfully, about water in gardens, remembering that the most memorable moments of my youthful rambles in the woods were those where I came unawares upon a little purling brook sliding cheerfully across mossy stones with ferns leaning over it. I spent enormous amounts of time looking into the possibilities; but the investment in supplies, labor, and maintenance and the fear of encouraging mosquitoes—which did not seem to need any encouragement—daunted me. Besides, a purling brook might be a bit out of keeping with the generally dry and windswept character of the landscape. I somehow didn't think that lushness was even to be aimed at. And looking back, I think I was probably right. In my next incarnation I do want a brook and a pond and water lilies and marsh marigolds and all those things. But that will be a different kind of place altogether.

I became acquainted with the idea of a garden that was a

series of rooms or places leading one on to ever new mini-environments—here a bit of open "meadowland," there a ferny dell, beyond a rocky outcrop overgrown by (suitably controlled) creepers. This corresponded exactly to something in me that was childish but heartfelt; I was charmed by the notion of a whole series of little retreats, each different and each a place unto itself. Of course, on six-tenths of an acre one has to forgo things like a sizable stand of sequoias; but a miniature world has its appeal too. I learned a lot from books about Japanese gardening.

Little by little my ideas crystallized and I began to put them into practice. More often than not they failed, and then I would try to figure out whether this was because I hadn't done it right or because there was some reason why this particular idea was not workable for that particular space. Often it was the latter; and more and more I came to the philosophical view that the most convincing results of "natural" gardening were to be achieved by *letting* things happen and *encouraging* them to happen rather than *forcing* them to happen.

By the second summer I was a confirmed worker-on-the-land. On weekends, and for a month in the summer, I would get up at dawn and work for anywhere from five to twelve hours; and this intense level of activity continued for a number of years. That a high proportion of these efforts came to naught in the way of fulfillment of my original ideas I have never resented. I have come to realize that in gardening, as in fishing, the manifest results are the least important benefits of the activity. Just being there is what is important—"simply messing about" in your garden, smelling the good earth, pouring out what our family calls mother juice (it was good to have another outlet for my nurturant nature, my children being now well along in adolescence). What is important is the dreaming and the planning, and the seeing it in one's mind's eye, so much more glorious than it ever is in reality.

One never sees one's garden as it is *this* year. There are occasional small triumphs, but the overall effect is never quite what you had in mind—or if it is, you have a new idea in mind by now. Those campanulas look too spotty, they should be grouped closer together. Wouldn't a bit of pink be good at the end of this arrangement? That lovely, dark mysterious corner would be even more satisfying with a small silvery-white something in its depths, reflecting the light and pointing up the darkness. Let's get rid of that intrusive branch at the corner of the path; it distracts your attention just when you should be focusing on the expanding woodland vista.

A person who is preoccupied with such imaginings and spends significant amounts of time trying to bring them to realization must, I think, be considered a gardener, and from this period I so considered myself. Against all expectation and all intention the metamorphosis had occurred.

The Gravel Pit—My Kindergarten

I have mentioned that the lower part of the property ended at
a road that was itself raised to counteract a natural hollow.
Our driveway, of course, had to be similarly raised to get over
this gully, and on one side the gully was filled in with a mixture
of rocks and subsoil over a square area about twenty feet on a
side to support the road. This was the Gravel Pit—and a good
name for it too. On this unpromising ground there has developed, over twenty years, the artless but agreeable spot my
grandchildren call "Grandma's Secret Garden"; to me, it will
always be the Gravel Pit.

There it sat, raw from the bulldozer. It was demarcated
from the driveway by a row of ugly and unmatching rocks that

I regretted as soon as they had been placed; on the other side, the area ended in a "cliff" consisting of even larger boulders that had been put there as a retaining wall. There was a small cedar tree at the driveway corner and another at the lower end of the "cliff"; to the north, the cedar-covered hillside began.

The first summer I ignored it. The second summer I planted one small pot of a pink flowering sedum and one of creeping thyme. I brought from the dump a bit of club moss and stuck it beside one of the rocks and commanded the Gravel Pit to flourish and bloom. It didn't. Time went by.

After I had been reading for a while, I began to visualize this space more seriously as a beautiful little garden, a sheltered hidey-hole far from the house and protected from the driveway and road by some sort of hedge. I created a step down into it with two flat stones, as a suitable entrance, and there I spent much of the next three summers making one mistake after another. There I learned, in fact, how *not* to garden in Rhode Island, and took thereby my first baby steps toward wisdom.

My first idea was to make the Gravel Pit into a kind of flowering meadow or alpine scree; the soil certainly looked poor and stony enough. I encouraged the little yellow-flowered cinquefoil that had appeared spontaneously, and I scattered seeds of all kinds of low-growing wild-looking flowers. What came up was grass. On all our excursions into the surrounding countryside I brought along pails and a shovel and trowel in the back of the station wagon and carried home daisies and buttercups and a little gray feltlike ground cover (which turned out to be a veronica), bird's-foot trefoil and Deptford pinks and wild pinks. The first year, in my ignorance, I even planted some sheep sorrel, thinking its rosettes were rather pretty. I have never ceased to regret it; to this day I spend an hour or two each

June getting every last root out of the ground, only to have it spring up again as lively as ever in August.

Practically all of my wildlings died, probably from lack of water as much as anything else. In this part of the world, July and August are essentially rainless except for thundershowers (which do more harm than good to little struggling things). It was a long way down the hill from the house, and at that time we had no hose long enough to reach all that distance. So water had to be carried down in a bucket, and I was too busy planting other things to do that very often. But I had some stern Puritan notion that since these were wild plants they ought to survive all by themselves without being coddled. Nobody had coddled them where I found them, had they? They were flourishing there, weren't they? Just because I moved them twenty miles or so was no reason for them to go into a decline. But they did go into a decline, most of them, and instead of a bevy of multi-colored flowers dancing in the breeze I had, at the end of several years, a Gravel Pit with occasional minute, sick and straggly, obviously homesick and miserable single wisps of plants.

Meanwhile the pink flowering sedum and creeping thyme I had originally planted had taken hold and made a bit of progress, and I had begun to learn (from all those books) the basic elements of handling plants, though I was still quite reluctant to do everything I was told to do—it just seemed like a great deal of work. But my unwillingness to proceed in the approved way wasn't getting me anywhere, so I compromised. I broke the little sedum and thyme plantings up into bite-sized portions and redistributed them over the whole area, but this time I made a little planting-hole for each piece and put in some compost (by this time I had compost), and watered the hole before and after planting. After a long dry spell, I would even bring down buck-

15

ets of water once in a while. Single small pots of a yellow-flowering sedum, and thrift (both from a New York City nursery), and a bit of Ajuga given me by a friend, and a little Arabis from a mail order catalog I broke up and spread around in the same way. As time went by I added a bit of gray woolly thyme, and strove diligently to eliminate several of the very weeds I had introduced in the first place.

Eventually the Gravel Pit was decently clothed in a ground-hugging patchwork mat, including a good deal of the thick soft club moss; and for some time now it has looked quite respectable, as long as I keep it weeded of grass and the ever-springing sheep sorrel. The sedums and the thyme blossom in their season, but mildly, not enough to spoil the illusion that this is a "naturally occurring" open space. It really is a kind of secret garden, and is where I habitually drink my morning coffee in three seasons of the year, sitting on one of the stones next to the driveway. Or did until the stone, over the years, grew unaccountably harder.

Gradually, I have made various improvements to this little room. The hideous mismatched rocks by the driveway are now almost entirely hidden (except for the one I sit on) by a barberry hedge—which is fine as long as I keep it reasonably pruned and free of bittersweet. Its red berries hang on all winter and brighten the driveway entrance (they also make wonderful indoor decorations for Christmas). For a privacy hedge along the road, after bayberry refused to perform, I planted a small slip of rugosa rose torn from an enormous stand on the beach; it revels in the poor, dry soil and is now eighteen feet long, six feet high, and still expanding.

At the top of the curving steps that lead from the Gravel Pit down into the Wild Garden, there is a nice little patch of evergreen candytuft, which also blooms in its season along with the grape hyacinths and scillas that are pretty freely scattered around. Arabis, in a now sizable planting along the northern edge, comes into bloom even before that, in a cloud of small white blossoms punctuated by two clumps of miniature daffodils. And in the northeast corner, where the Gravel Pit abuts against the hill, is a bit of what I think of as "thickening" or "foaming"—places where one might expect the soil to have become deeper and richer over the years, and to hold moisture better, and therefore to support somewhat more lushness than in the rest of the area. This process had actually begun in that particular corner, and I began to see wild columbine and butter-cups blooming away where I had never planted them. So I helped it along by digging out (well, asking my son-in-law to dig out) the corner for a few feet and planting, for a continuous sequence of bloom, a few each of daffodils, wild iris ("blue flag"), fringed bleeding heart, evening primroses, native daylilies, black-eyed Susan, and blue roadside asters. A few foxgloves have decided to join the party and appear in different locations every year, as do the tall yellow mulleins. This little corner, though no more than eight or ten feet square, presents a nice "bouquet" of color through most of the summer, which livens the room and gives it a focus without detracting from its general air of simplicity and greenness.

I have, as you may have noticed, a special fondness for the Gravel Pit. Hardly anyone else comes there, and no one else actually sits there and spins dreams as I do. Maybe I have been a little too successful in achieving the natural look, and they think it just happened to be a pretty spot. But I remember it when it was literally nothing. It is my creation, and I love what I have made.

Getting Outfitted

I had not been working outside for long before I realized that garments used for my kind of gardening could not be worn for anything else. When I garden, I mingle very closely with the elements of my craft, including soil and compost. Juicy plants that stain are clasped to my breast to be carried up or down the hill; thorns attack me (and my clothes) from all sides; my shoes are immersed in substances that are delicious in themselves but not acceptable in the living quarters. Besides these considerations, I found I needed protection from sun (usually), cold and wind (sometimes), poison ivy (always, and mostly when you don't expect it), ticks (from May through July), mosquitoes, and ants. When I tried to research this subject I found almost no information, and it really would have been useful to me in the days of my first ignorance; so I include it here in the hope that you too are looking for advice and will find it helpful.

At the time I started doing this kind of work, down in the Gravel Pit, women's trousers could not properly be called *slacks*; they were definitely *taut*, all the way from waist to ankle, with no ease anywhere, and the fabric usually included a high proportion of polyester. These pants were hot to wear, impossible to move or sit on the ground in, and just not businesslike. So for a long period I wore men's work shirt-and-pants outfits, ordered from a uniform supply catalog. These had enough polyester not to wrinkle, and looked quite dapper (at that stage, I was still interested in how I looked while gardening). They had numerous large pockets and were cut so as to allow plenty of movement; they wore like iron, and they were amazingly cheap. In fact, they had only one major fault: since they were meant for men, if the hips were big enough the waist was tremendous, so there was a certain amplitude of material around the middle. But they served me well for years until I found out, by accident, how much cooler pure cotton is, and how much more comfortable *very* loose, nondapper garments are.

By that time women's trousers were starting to be made with plenty of front pleats, an excellent thing for a woman with plenty of front. When this fashion reached its peak I acquired a lifetime supply of pleated cotton canvas pants two sizes bigger than my usual street wear, with a series of extremely loose, even billowing, cotton shirts made of canvas or, for hot days, thin twill. The pants, being cut for women, don't have to be belted in to stay on—in fact, my favorite ones are designed without any belt, just a fitted yoke; this again makes for great freedom of movement.

To complete the outfit I wear a brimmed hat that comes well down over my eyes, loose enough to be worn a long time with comfort but snug enough not to blow off too easily; heavy cotton socks; and loose ankle-high "desert boots" of unlined suede, to keep out dirt and compost and ants. I give these shoes no care whatever and they last (once I've replaced the cotton laces with leather ones) for years and years.

Mind you, these clothes do not *look* good. The material of the pants and shirts stains and wrinkles, and everything is so loose that the general effect is like that of Jackie Coogan in *The Kid*, or an ancient, unadorable big-city derelict. But I have been, for some years now, well past caring about that, and I work in comfort.

The same clothes serve for winter work, with the progressive addition of a cotton or silk turtleneck and a down vest and denim jacket on top, and long underpants of silk or fleece on the bottom. An extra pair of wool socks over the cotton ones helps too, and a wool cap under or instead of the brimmed hat. The work one does in winter tends to be strenuous and heat-producing; after an initial warm-up you find yourself shedding a surprising number of layers as you go along.

I always bring gloves along to whatever part of the grounds I'm working in. The pretty cotton trifles sold as "gardening gloves" are no good at all; they wear through in less than a week. Besides, for a great deal of my work I need thorn protection and/or good solid poison ivy protection; for this, men's heavy leather-palmed gloves are adequate but far too bulky and inconvenient for any but the grossest jobs. The best gloves for my purposes—and they're so comfortable I've begun wearing them for almost all my weeding and digging as well as for brush-cutting—are the expensive but wonderful ones made of goatskin, which are beautifully soft and made in women's sizes that actually fit. They cost six times as much as the cotton ones, and last ten times as long.

(I recognize—with no sense of *moral* superiority—that if you are under thirty-five you are going to go out there in skin-tight shorts and sandals and a low-cut sleeveless vest, bareheaded in all weathers, cheerfully enduring the sunburn and the chapping, the thorns and the slivers and the poison ivy, with your hair falling in your face and bugs all over you. You will take this in stride and look marvelous doing it and feel none the worse the next day, and that is how we know you *are* under thirty-five. By all means keep it up as long as you can. When you decide you would prefer to be comfortable, reread this chapter.)

I use only a few tools. For digging up new areas I rely on a spading fork instead of a shovel because I find it much handier to work between and around the multiple stones of all sizes that constitute this soil. Being no stronger than is becoming for a woman of my age, I couldn't hoist any significant number of shovelfuls of soil anyway. Even for bulbs I have to get down there and dig; those nice cylindrical "bulb planters" they show in the catalogs just grind to an immediate halt in most of the places I want to put bulbs. My system is to loosen up a small area by prodding and prying with the spading fork, remove the stones into a bucket (or two) and haul them away, come back with the bucket full of compost, and mix it in with a trowel. If I'm planting fairly large things, I loosen up and de-stone *two* layers before adding the compost; this gives me a twelve-inch depth of good planting soil, which is about as much as I ever do by myself.

My trowel is made of cast aluminum, and came in a set with a slimmer brother (meant for bulb planting, but too small) and a sturdy hand fork that I almost never use. All other trowels rust, or bend, or come to pieces under stress, or hurt your hand; this one has stood up to ten years of hard service already and is functionally as good as new, although considerably pitted in its surface.

The weeding tool I swear by is one I have never seen advertised or described *as* a weeding tool, but it has been my constant companion for fifteen years. Nothing else comes close to its usefulness. You get this treasure in a hardware store, where they call it a "tack puller." It is shaped a good deal like a screwdriver except that the business end is just slightly forked and just slightly curved—so as to insinuate neatly under the tack, I suppose. (It is interesting, to me, that garden stores do sell a nearly identical instrument for getting up deep-rooted things like dandelions, but that is anywhere from eighteen inches to three feet long and is meant to be used from a standing position. It's very good for that purpose, but impossibly unhandy to use for little bits of things, while sitting or kneeling on the ground.) For any weed that won't come up root and all with the fingers alone, I use this to loosen the soil and get right down under the bulb or the main root ball, whence an easy levering motion brings the whole thing up into the light and into my waiting pail.

I have not found a hoe to be helpful, since none of my plants grow in rows and most of the ground has some kind of ground cover on it. I carry with me, always, hand pruning shears, and usually longer-handled loppers as well (I can't get any woody stem over about half an inch with the hand shears, and not even that diameter of the very tough cedar wood).

For heavier pruning, which I do less frequently, I take very long-handled, very strong clippers, and a small saw. (Warning: Excessive heavy sawing, especially if you're not quite strong enough for the job, can give you a painful and recurrent bursitis of the shoulder. Either work up to such exercise gradually over several weeks, to develop the muscle you need, or get somebody else to do it.)

I have a beautiful wheelbarrow and it would probably be very useful in a normal garden, but our place is so hilly and rough that I find it awkward to handle. For me, two large plastic pails are just right for carrying weeds to the compost pile and compost back to the planting area. A smaller pail nested inside holds my tools and gloves to and from the work area. These are perhaps individual preferences, but I've tried other ways and this works for me.

Increasingly, working on our sandy, stony ground, I have taken to the luxury of a hard-rubber kneeling pad, which holds up surprisingly well. A variant has the pad attached to a metal frame that converts to a seat when stood on its head; its handles help you lift and lower yourself. So far I find this not necessary, and awkward to haul around; but I may come to it yet. Rubber pads that strap around your knees or slip into pockets in your pants are, in my experience, never in just the right spot when you need them, so that you find yourself coming down confidently with all your weight onto some excruciating small sharp stone.

For a number of years I kept a detailed garden notebook that included a section describing what I had done day by day and hour by hour, and another section listing plants or seeds to be ordered, garden "effects" good or bad in various locations, chores to be done at another season ("divide Hyperion," "move seedling foxgloves to corner of house"). These notes made enjoyable reading in the winter and were sometimes useful in reminding me of what I had planted where, but I found them

24

otherwise not worth the extensive time it took to write them up, and stopped doing it.

I still tend to make lists but that is more because I am a list maker by temperament than for any practical purpose, since I seldom refer to the lists once they are written. When I go out into the garden to work, the top-priority jobs clamor for immediate attention and it is rare indeed that I have any need, or time, to consult a written list to see what is next to be done. (The elegant, tightly organized and beautifully illustrated "garden notebooks" available from catalogs are fun to leaf through, but no good for writing in; if you do go in for a notebook, it should be one based on your own system, not someone else's.)

I do, of course, make diagrams of planting areas that are relatively complex, to be sure I have considered relationships of height, form, color, and seasonal change. The extent to which I indulge myself in this kind of planning and the elaborateness with which I am willing to develop it are astonishing, though about eighty percent is lost in the translation to the real garden. I have concluded that the conception in the gardener's head is an art form of one kind and the creation of an actual picture out of living plant material is an art form of quite another kind. Both are satisfying, but their relationship to each other is, in my experience, tenuous.

Whether or not to label your plants is a decision that should be made early in your gardening career. It is certainly helpful, if you want to replace or extend a successful planting, to know exactly what species and variety you are dealing with (assuming that the nursery where you got them originally had identified them correctly, which can't be taken entirely for granted). And for certain personalities there is an intrinsic satisfaction in knowing exactly what one has and even from what nursery it came.

But I personally don't like the mechanical look of labels all over my garden. Also, I've found that most labels fade or disintegrate within a few seasons, so that to be sure of a correct identification you either have to keep a written record indoors somewhere or invest in metal labels with the plant name and variety punched in. In general I don't do either of these, and am occasionally sorry for it.

There are two situations when I do use labels: to show where bulbs are planted, when I'm planning to put in other plants several months later; and conversely, to show the location of existing plants when I'm planning to put bulbs near or among them in the fall when they may be unrecognizable. Both of these uses are temporary, and plain plastic labels (or even wooden tongue depressors from the drugstore) are adequately sturdy. Write on these labels with a soft pencil, not a pen.

What comes next is a practical point that I have found enormously helpful; it concerns the way one's work is organized. The issue is certainly of minor importance to a vigorous gardener of twenty-two, but for anyone whose energy or enthusiasm (or back) is at all limited it is well worth while to break work projects up into twenty- or thirty-minute sections and alternating stand-up with sit-down jobs, heavy carrying with fidgety fine weeding, and so on. Among other advantages, this prevents you from scamping the work just because you or your muscles are tired of a given activity; simply moving to a different part of the garden and using a different set of muscles gives considerable refreshment and renewed energy. The same amount of work gets done in the end, and there is really no need for succumbing to that grim sense of "I *have* to *finish* this job *today*" when your fingers are in spasm and your concentration has dissipated.

Similarly, it makes sense to work in shady areas on a hot day and in sunny areas on a cold day, and to do light work in the heat and heavy work in the cold. These maxims seem ridiculously obvious now but *I* didn't think of them until I'd been gardening for some years. The general principle is to apply your energy to work that needs it (of which there is always plenty), not to squander it in unnecessary heroics.

West Bank Story

Our house was built on a level space created by digging into a hillside, and as always in such cases there were steep banks, on the north and west sides as it happened, to contend with. That on the west was a good thirty feet long, eight feet high at the back of the house, and it sloped down to join the lawn at the front. This bank, when we moved in, was quite naked and in obvious danger from erosion, so I gave some immediate attention to the subject of bank plantings.

Low-growing junipers were the logical and best solution, but were at that time out of the question economically. So, after appropriate research, I put in a considerable planting of crown vetch, which was said to be a useful soil binder for slopes, extensively used on highways. It looked very pretty in the pictures.

It was a good soil binder, just as advertised. And it was pretty, just as advertised—when it was in bloom, which was for about a month in midsummer. After that it looked like an un- kempt tangle until frost, when it looked dead and had to be cut away, leaving a noneroding but visually naked bank again. This was no good.

I read a good deal about bank gardens and, in the lower reaches of this bank, built several little terraces made of small rocks, and installed what the books assured me were suitable plants—things like cheddar pink and moss pink and *Saponaria ocymoides splendens* (whose name still entrances me) and a whole slew of others. They didn't find the bank to their liking, and either died or sulked interminably. Then I learned about Doro- thy Perkins roses, those ubiquitous pink clamberers that cover railroad embankments all over this part of the country. Waiting for trains back to New York, I investigated the local station. Sure enough, Dorothy Perkins roses galore. In the dusk of summer evenings, before the arrival of the eight o'clock train into the city, I snipped off growing tips and laboriously rooted them and grew them on (those were the years when I had a greenhouse—of which more later). In a couple of years I had half a dozen nice little plants and set them out on my still unclothed bank.

No go. They didn't die and they didn't do anything worth living for.

In the meantime I had, as a desperate temporizing measure, seeded all the lower reaches of the bank with another creeping thyme (reasoning that in my dry, unsterile soil thyme was just what the doctor ordered). It was not enthusiastic but it did eventually come along and provide coverage of a sort. But by that time I had started still another effort, consisting of half a dozen *Cotoneaster dammeri* in the center top of the bank. This was in the sixth or seventh year of our residence and we were getting pretty tired of that completely unsatisfactory planting, which was a real eyesore. These cotoneasters (which for several years I pronounced "cotton Easters," until an embarrassing confrontation at the local nursery taught me the correct "co-TONE-ee-aster") were, I thought, a forlorn hope, because the books talked very ominously about something called fire blight, which could strike at any time and destroy an entire planting.

But I took very good care of them, keeping them watered and weeded and smothering them twice a year with all the compost they could possibly digest, weighting the ends of their little branches down with stones to encourage them to put out new roots, and generally treating them like beloved invalid children. And along about the third year, lo and behold, they took fire or struck gold or were touched by the Spirit, and began to spread over the bank in all directions, smothering thyme and pinks and weeds. If allowed, I think that cotoneaster would have taken over the whole lawn. It gives a pleasantly textured surface to the bank and has pretty, inconspicuous white flowers in the spring and has never shown any disease at all, let alone fire blight; so I am very happy with it and don't even mind the yearly chore of trimming its hair.

That's the lower part of the bank, the part to the south. The whole bank is too long a stretch, I've always thought, to be planted with just one thing; it requires a little variety and incident to keep it from looking institutional. About in the center, accordingly, I have put one huge plant of the rockspray cotoneaster, a big arching thing, which never amounted to much until its little brother *dammeri* got going, and now seems determined to show it who's boss by throwing out sprays five and six feet long—perhaps a bit too much incident for the site, I'm going to start reproving it any day now. Above it, right on the top of the bank, sits a thriving clump of pink heather left over from the days when it was going to be a "planted wall." It blooms violently from December to March and provides delightful little nosegays for the house in the winter months.

Then there are two dwarf weeping hemlocks, very beautiful in my opinion, though not as dwarf as they once were. I found one in the faithful North Stonington dump, along with another one near it, which I thought was the same thing but which after a period of some years revealed its intention of becoming a full-sized forest tree. By the time it got to eight feet high it looked positively menacing in its top heaviness and obvious vigor and I most reluctantly cut it down (there was *no* place on our property for such a conspicuous monster, so beautiful but so definitely weird). The other dwarf weeper I ordered from a nursery to keep the first one company; they provide a nice billowy accent of softer green among the darkness and twigginess of the cotoneaster.

The northern third of the bank is still not very satisfactory. It is nominally planted with low junipers, but this has been done piecemeal as other things have died off and my ideas have changed, so not all the junipers match (I buy them locally and am often not sure of the exact variety I'm getting). In addition, one particular group of eight plants came along well for a while and then went into a decline over a period of several years; I thought this was due to smothering by the Confederate violets that for some reason adore that bank; they grow ten and twelve inches tall and shade everything underneath their four-inch leaves. But then the juniper planting in a nearby location also died off, and the nursery man told me that both were suffering from a blight, against which there was no recourse. So finally they were pulled out and replaced, bringing us back to square one. Someday, I feel sure, that end of the slope will fill in and mellow, but for me it has been as nearly incorrigible as any place on the property.

The West Rock—a Small Success

On the top of the West Bank, running the full length of the house, is an open slope about fifteen feet wide, terminating in the brush that denotes the property line in this area. Our very first family picnic on this land, just after we had become its owners, took place on that slope—it made a good vantage point for gazing at the whole extent of our new domain. And my eye was caught, immediately, by one of those enormous rounded granite rocks. This one was about four by ten feet, with an interesting bend in its waist and a smaller rock apparently glued on top as an afterthought.

Even at first sight this arrangement struck me as crying out for development, and it actually became the subject of one of my first little landscaping efforts. The fact that it constitutes the focus of the main view from our bedroom window helped to keep it in my mind and to stimulate my best endeavors, and I have been pleased with the result.

The rock lies at the foot of a young wild cherry tree, which overhangs it attractively. I keep the tree pruned pretty well back so that it doesn't overwhelm the scene or keep it too shaded. For the planting in the bend of the rock, I used a good sprinkling of Mount Hood daffodils which are pure white, interplanted them quite thickly with balloon flower, and carpeted the whole thing with vinca. In the creases and irregularities near the top of the rock, where there seems to be another one perching, I cleaned out the accumulated cedar needles and debris and packed in sifted compost, in which I started a bit of gray curly sedum with a bright pink September bloom. At the shallow lower end of the rock where there was already a formation vaguely resembling a miniature scree, I infiltrated the gravel with more compost and put more sedum.

This little picture is even milder and simpler in appearance than the description may sound; to the casual observer, it is not noticeable that any deliberate planting has been done around the rock. But through the year there is a succession of gentle, agreeable changes that keep the view from the window moving with the seasons.

More has been added, with time. I had a pathetic little twig of a wild azalea, *Rhododendron nudiflorum*, from a Woolworth's store in New York City. This was in my first year here; I knew nothing except that azaleas were supposed to be pretty. I paid, I think, about seventy-five cents for it (it was all of four inches high at the time) and tried it in various places of honor around the edge of our lawn but it failed to be pretty—in fact, it almost failed to grow and usually failed to bloom. But still . . . it was

an azalea; I couldn't possibly do away with it. Finally I noticed, on a shopping trip into town, a wild azalea growing naturally by the roadside. I stopped and investigated; it was the same as mine. So I noted very carefully its exact location and exposure and surroundings and neighbors, and came home and put mine in as nearly the same situation as I could find on our land— which turned out to be the brush border on the western property line, within a few feet of the "West Rock." It has thrived there ever since.

Not that it's really that pretty: the pale naked stems look skimpy and shivery all winter, the flowers are a sickly mauve, and the leaves, which come right afterward, are a clashing yellowish green. But it's not very conspicuous as a shrub, being in back of other things, and it does bloom early which is nice, and not only is it an azalea, but its common name is Pinxterflower, which is, for me, irresistible; and finally, it is loyally willing to grow and bloom for me in spite of the abuse it suffered in early life, and that seems to create an obligation on my part.

My husband gave me an azalea from the florist one year, as an anniversary present. It was a particularly rich shade of deep red, and I immediately pictured it in my mind blooming in the shade to the west. As soon as its blossoms fell I planted it there, with an underplanting of pachysandra to keep our enthusiastic lawn boys from coming too close. It took to the spot and did so well that I repeated the process twice more in subsequent years, once with a pure white azalea and again with one of salmon pink. These are all evergreen and make a nice little colony to balance the vinca planting. After the daffodils have faded, the three azaleas bloom one after the other with just a little overlapping: first the red, then the white, and then the pink. This was not planned but it makes a very pleasant sequence, and keeps the view from the bedroom window interesting for a long time.

After the azaleas fade there is a hiatus as far as flowers are concerned, but the birdhouse on the wild cherry tree is invariably occupied by this time and the doings of the house-wren family as well as their beautiful singing keep the entertainment level well up. In July the balloonflowers start to show their big puffy buds and they bloom through much of August, a lovely cool periwinkle blue, quiet and refreshing in the midsummer heat. When they have gone and the stems have been cut back, the gray sedum puts out its pink blossoms, so unobtrusively that you have to be looking for them. And then the vinca takes over and the leaves of the wild cherry fall on it and everything rests until the next spring.

The Compost Pile

A long about my third year at this work, finding that my original uninstructed methods were producing excellent compost for all my purposes, I came to the conclusion that there is a lot of nonsense in the books about the "correct" way to make this lovely stuff; at least, it's nonsense for the average amateur gardener. You can buy, through catalogs and garden centers, expensive "compost bins" and other containers, and packets of scientifically grown bacteria to speed the process— you would think this was a really esoteric undertaking. All, in my opinion, nonsense. Compost has its own bacteria all by itself, and it doesn't need a special container. Even in the smallest backyard, there can be spared a space eight or ten feet square, screened off with a fence or vine. As for speeding the process, that's only important the first year; after that there is a never-ending supply, and what does it matter if what you're using is what was laid down a year ago rather than three months ago?

My system has indeed, like the compost itself, ripened over time, and I think it is now hardly to be improved on. My compost pile is in the northwest part of the property, behind a large wild cherry tree and further screened by a thicket of honeysuckle bushes, heavily infested with bittersweet. I chose the spot because it was out of the way and also because there was a natural depression there. The available open area is roughly ten feet across, and the compost heap is in the form of a fat doughnut occupying most of this space. The circle of the doughnut is broken at one point, which is my working area; this point moves progressively round and round the doughnut clockwise from right to left.

As I fill up my big pails with weeded, pinched, and pruned material, I bring them up and empty them at the "new" end (on my right), and when I need compost I shovel or trowel it out from the "old" end (on my left); whatever tough stems or roots are not yet sufficiently rotted are thrown back to the right for further processing. (It is usual to find that the entire exterior surface of the pile shows little modification and needs more "cooking"; only inside, where the necessary heat for chemical and bacterial action has been developed, do you come to the gold.)

At the beginning of a new growing season, the doughnut is nearly complete; but as the spring advances and I install new plantings and put thick layers of compost on the established ones, I make rapid inroads and normally reduce it by half, using up pretty much all the fully decomposed material. If I finish the spring work and still haven't used it all up, I store it in two enormous plastic trash cans that stand right there, where it serves me conveniently all through the summer and fall. (Being as much of a procrastinator as the next person, I often don't get around to this and just keep nibbling away at the left-hand end every time I need compost; but it is a thrifty and luxurious feeling to have it sorted out and stored away.) As the summer progresses, more and more material gets added to the right-hand end; by the end of November the circle is nearly complete again, and about four feet high, compacting down over the winter to two feet or so.

I don't make scientific layers, as they tell you to; but I do make some attempt to alternate very coarse, dry material like goldenrod stems with very fine, moist material like chickweed or ferns. (Woody stems and branches take too long to turn into compost; they go on a separate brush pile, which is periodically shredded and taken away to the landfill). I don't shovel on layers of soil either; but when I bring up a couple of buckets of weeds with nice clumps of soil clinging to their roots, or sods from a new planting place, I try to place them over a "dry" area that doesn't seem to have much soil.

I don't water the compost at all, but I do take some pains to keep the sides fairly vertical and the top shaped with a slight central trough so as to retain rain. I don't turn the compost or aerate it in any way, and I don't add any lime or other fertilizing agent. Nor do I put kitchen waste on the pile because, the one summer I did, dogs and raccoons tore it apart repeatedly and made messes (though a friend of mine says she buries her kitchen waste in her compost pile in tightly closed paper bags and has no trouble with marauders).

If I did all the "correct" things I don't do, I would probably get faster and *maybe*, in certain respects, better compost. But my method is simple and easy, and it supplies me with enough rich, dark, fine, well-rotted, odorless compost for nearly all my needs both indoors and out. Only for planting large shrubs and trees does the nurseryman have to bring in peat moss, and even then I generally add a heavy ring of compost on the top when he has finished, and repeat it twice a year until the newcomer is well started.

Located as it is under a canopy of tree and shrub branches, the compost pile is a cool and agreeable place to work, but there is one disadvantage: the tree and the shrubs (and bittersweet vines) dearly love the additional nutrition, and send their roots foraging through the pile with great enthusiasm. The wild cherry tree, in fact, which was noticeably old and failing when we arrived, has taken a new lease on life and is the biggest, healthiest wild cherry on our grounds now. And the bittersweet and honeysuckle have to be cut back hard every year, just to give me room to move.

But the worst problem is that the roots of these things penetrate the compost so thoroughly and tightly that it is a major ordeal to winnow them out. Besides slowing the process of harvesting the compost enormously (often I have to loosen it up a few forkfuls at a time and then sit down and laboriously sift it with my fingers, handful by handful, to untangle and remove the roots), much of the stored nutrient goodness, I suspect, has gone into those roots and what remains is relatively nonhelpful from a nutritional point of view, though still useful as a physical "conditioner" of my sandy soil. Pondering on this subject over the years with increasing rancor, I came eventually upon the idea of lining the bottom and sides of the depression that holds the compost pile with two-to-three-foot lengths of board, placed close enough together to prevent the vast majority of roots from nosing through, but still allowing drainage and earthworm migration and so on. I did this paving gradually as I worked my way around the ring. This arrangement has been amazingly effective: now I can shovel out the new compost freely with almost no root interference, and my time in the compost pile has been cut by about 80 percent. This was one of my better ideas.

As to other nutrients: I don't normally add any lime to my garden, even though my soil is intensely acid (my husband uses a great deal of lime on the lawn). What does grow here seems to accept the acidity without complaint, and I really don't want the trouble of catering to the individual pH requirements of each plant I have. Moreover, it would seem that many of my plants don't know their own pH requirements, and flourish under conditions that the books describe as unfavorable. I also use almost no inorganic fertilizer, partly because I really don't want things to grow any faster or bigger than they do now. (I make an exception for my various roses, especially those that bloom more than once during the summer, and for the west side of the house, where I do strive for, though I've never achieved, some semblance of a "perennial border.")

I use bone meal when I plant new bulbs, and once a year (sometimes) thereafter when the new bulb shoots show, and all over the rock garden, scantily mixed into a one-inch layer of compost, in the early spring (again, sometimes). Otherwise my sole fertilizer is the compost itself, applied two inches thick to the west side of the house in spring and fall, and in similarly good, thick layers wherever things are not doing as well as I'd like or the soil is perceptibly wearing out under a bush or I have a relatively new planting that I want to coddle temporarily. This approach works very well for the look I want, which is that of a healthy landscape just slightly on the meager side, like the rest of Rhode Island.

Around the House

The house at Woodwinds has a very simple architecture, its only decoration being the wide deck that runs around three sides (south, east, and west). On the east side, the house (under the deck level) is shaded from even morning sun by a stand of cedar trees; on the south, the deck is ten feet wide so that in summer the sun only penetrates about halfway under it; and on the west, there is the high bank I have talked about, with shrubs and trees on its summit, effectively reducing the amount of direct sunshine here to just two or three hours. Obviously this has been a major opportunity for "gardening in the shade."

The first summer I planted ferns all around the house, and this is not a bad expedient, I still think, while one is mulling it all over. The ferns came from the North Stonington town dump, and included some good tall ones like ostrich and interrupted fern, so they made quite a respectable three-dimensional mass of greenery in short order. But of course they collapsed into a thin mass of soggy hay in the winter, and then the house looked naked and forlorn.

By the third summer I had enough confidence to dig up a sizable number of young mountain laurels, also from the dump. (I should have explained before that by the luckiest of circumstances the dump was at this time being enlarged and bulldozers were knocking down whole mountainsides of just the sort of plant material I wanted. I did get permission, and did my collecting under the very noses of the bulldozers.) I set them out in a single line all around the east and south sides, about a foot from the house wall. By the fourth summer, having been further educated, I moved them to three feet away from the walls (to let them expand more naturally, and to allow space for periodic housepainting), staggered them slightly, and grouped them for a less formal look, and underplanted them with pachysandra.

This arrangement has matured nicely and has been a general success. As individual mountain laurels have succumbed to old age, I have replaced them with other shade lovers: one *Rhododendron maximum*, two *Andromeda* side by side, and one American holly. (The reason I have not filled in the empty spaces, as they occur, with more mountain laurels is that the bulldozers finished their work in the dump and I don't know of any other place to scavenge such beautiful shrubs; I've tried buying them but have had poor luck.)

With regard to the holly: I was not *very* well educated at this point because I bought only a female plant and then forgot what specific kind of holly it was, so I've never been able to get a mate for the poor thing. (See, I should have labeled her, or at least kept a record of her family background.) She has grown mightily and bloomed hopefully season after season (she's on the southwest corner, where she does get a good bit of sun), but of course is quite unable to produce the Christmas berries I had counted on. Actually she is beginning to *look* like an old maid, somewhat scrawny and sour; I am currently trying to smother my guilt feelings and just give her up for a bad job and replace her with a fertile young couple. This is surprisingly hard (surprisingly for a rational human being) to do.

I note that the books say mountain laurel needs "no fertilizer, only a generous layer of oak leaves each autumn." Mine, after their initial planting in compost and an additional two pailfuls of compost each in the next year, have received no fertilizer and only what good they may get out of the occasional dropped leaves of the pachysandra. They look just fine and bloom furiously.

The west side of the house has been a problem. It's an unbroken stretch about thirty-five feet long, and it has been my dream to produce here a definitive if small "perennial border" of the kind the English gardening books describe so irresistibly. This result has so far escaped me, for reasons that I mostly don't understand. Of course I am aware that the area gets relatively little direct sun; but I have been careful to put in only shade-loving plants. And then it may be that the soil is just too acid; but I have, for several years in a row, added lime without any perceptible change. I know the soil is basically fertile; I've dug this border down to two full feet on two occasions, adding perfectly vast amounts of compost; and most years I give it an overall dressing of two inches of compost in the fall and again in the spring. It was once suggested to me that the problem might arise from toxic runoff from the stain we use for the outside house walls; but if that's the case, why is it no better five years after the last staining and no worse in the year immediately after staining? I am baffled; but of course I have never sent a soil sample to the state agricultural station because I like to be independent (even in areas where I'm incompetent), and to retain the sense that I'm doing it "all by myself"—that my garden and I communicate by secret, mystic affinities needing no intermediary. This attitude is irrational and sometimes seriously harmful, but it is part of the charm of gardening for me.

In the end, after much wastage of energy and plant material, I have come up with a few things that *will* grow and am sticking to them. What will grow, and very well too, is, first, a climbing rose called New Dawn, which has perfectly lovely fragrant shell-pink blooms. It is true that this, which is reputed to be a repeat bloomer, has never given me a single blossom after its first tremendous show in late June. But it climbs very nicely up to deck level and then spreads for a good fifteen feet in both directions, mingling on the southwest corner of the deck with the wisteria. Because (I suppose) of the relative lack of light at ground level there are no blooms at all until it hits the second floor, so my idea of having roses peeking in the window of the ground floor bedroom on that corner has never been fulfilled. But the show from the living room window just above is spectacular.

At the southern corner of this border is a magenta-flowered spirea that turned up in the Gravel Pit, the very first year we were here, as a two-inch seedling blooming its little head off. Without having any idea of what it was, but thrilled by the fact that something in my garden was actually blossoming, I immediately transferred it to the house corner, where it has done very well ever since, asking only to have its deadwood cut back every spring. Its major bloom comes in July but it continues to show a respectable number of new blossoming tips well through August; thus it maintains a sort of definitive color statement at that end of the house.

At the other end I had for many years a lilac bush; but, like the climbing rose, it only bloomed on its upper branches, which leaned wistfully toward the west in a manner to break your heart; also, its roots would not allow anything else to survive within four feet of the main trunk, which interfered with the effect of my so carefully planned balance of bloom. Finally I took it down and planted in its place a group of royal hostas, which make a good terminal statement all summer and bloom—majestically—in August.

Aside from these big things, which form as it were the backbone of the planting, the mainstays have been various daylilies; astilbe in pink, red, and white; Madonna lilies in the spring (you would expect a "Madonna lily" to be squeamish about soil and location, but they're perfectly vigorous and very beautiful); a creeping bellflower (*Campanula ranunculoides*) that I found growing by the roadside in a huge stand (it's the roots that creep—the stems are three feet high); some varicolored columbines that grew from seed I collected in the garden of a Swedish friend; some of the local wild asters; and an especially thick and vivid goldenrod called Seaside Goldenrod, one of the few that is still good-looking in close-up.

Among them all they provide reasonable bloom during most of the summer months, and the planting as a whole looks "quite all right" (an expression our family uses for damning with faint praise). But oh, the wonderful compositions I have planned and planted and nurtured that have gone and left no trace! When I tell you that daffodils and bee balm and the native lythrum die out after a couple of years, and the supposedly foolproof aster Wonder of Staffa has failed three times, you will (if you have any gardening experience at all) realize that this little patch of soil really does have a curse on it.

An adjunct to this border is the wisteria that twines up the westernmost deck post and from there spreads out in two directions over the railings. On the west side of the house it meets and mingles with the New Dawn rose, and on the south side it races along the whole thirty-four-foot length of the deck and plunges joyously into the cedar tree that rises up at the far corner, climbing in a given summer another fifteen or twenty feet. This vine blooms so beautifully in June that the deck is a veritable bower, and even at other times it somehow clothes and naturalizes the house on its whole southern aspect; so I don't begrudge it the four extensive prunings it needs each year to keep it from taking over the whole deck. Actually its expansiveness turned out to be an advantage when our new neighbors to the west built their house quite close to the property line and in such a way that the two decks, theirs and ours, were within close view of each other. We simply added a couple of layers to the existing deck railing so that it rose eight feet into the air, trained the willing wisteria around the new rails, and in two seasons had a visually impenetrable screen that still lets some breeze come through.

At the foot of the deck post where the wisteria is planted there lies a largish, flattish rock, and near it, so as to make a kind of grouping with the wisteria, is a Betty Prior rose. I can't speak too highly of this lady. Not only has she competed successfully with those rampaging wisteria roots for a good fifteen years now, but she blooms absolutely incessantly from early June to well beyond Thanksgiving, with single scarlet blooms that get progressively darker and brighter in tone as the nights get colder. She has withstood complete neglect for a couple of years at a time, and perfectly fierce pruning at other times; and as far as I can see, she's as good as new. Her flowers are of a color that is particularly pretty against the green lawn, especially in the yellow light of late afternoon, and especially in late October, when there's nothing else in bloom in that area.

The Wild Garden

O ur entire property slopes fairly steeply from north to south. Below the patch of artificially leveled lawn to the south of the house, there is a real hillside, which on our arrival was occupied by a mature collection of red cedars, with a scanty undergrowth of arrowwood, bayberry, and bush honeysuckle, and brambles well interlaced throughout. In one sizable area there was a solid thicket, fifteen feet high, of poison ivy; this place, which now accommodates a nice seating arrangement on a little terrace, I still call Poison Ivy Plaza. Toward the west the slope was relatively more open, with one ancient shadbush reaching for the sun.

For the first two or three years, occupied with other matters, I occasionally squirmed my way into the outskirts of this jungle and thought about its possibilities. Nothing grandiose, nothing that involved earth moving, ever entered my mind; whatever was going to be done would be doable by my own effort, with whatever occasional help I could scrounge from my rapidly growing children. And clearly that would not be a whole lot. So, obviously, this was going to remain a Wild Garden. Fortunately a Wild Garden was exactly what I wanted.

My first job was to clear out Poison Ivy Plaza, which turned out to be fairly easy to do: those towering gnarled stalks, laden with bunches of berries from years past, were readily cut down to about four feet from the ground and the remainder, I learned with relief, could be pulled up with only a reasonable amount of exertion, along with several feet of shaggy root. This clearing took several days and seemed to me a tremendous accomplishment. I still remember the sweltering July afternoon (it happened to be my forty-ninth birthday) when I staggered into the room where my clean, kempt family was gathered to give me a party and announced, sweating and beaming from every pore, "I have killed the dragon!" (Postscript: Not quite. There are to this day a few remnants of poison ivy that need pulling up every time I weed the area—which I do only about once a year, so they keep having time to get another good start. But basically it is under control.)

For the rest of that summer I sat in Poison Ivy Plaza eating my lunches and staring around at the steepness of the slope, the tangled overgrowth of honeysuckle, the total absence of anything calming or refreshing, any harmony of color or shape, anything at all pleasing to any of the senses. Greenness per se was no longer enough for me; I wanted a Wild Garden, but it had to be a Garden.

So I turned it into a Garden in a series of stages, the first being the creation of paths. By the time I made them I had clambered around the hillside enough to have some idea of how I was going to organize it, and also to understand (by experience) the natural and necessary ways of getting from one place to another. I myself cleared the brush and brambles from the pathways and my good son who was home from school that summer put in three-foot lengths of cedar trunk (saved from the clearing made for the house) for steps. A few years later, when these began to rot to the point of being dangerous, a couple of strong biddable high-school boys came and replaced the cedar steps with nice stone stepping-stones, collected during the intervening time from all over the property. Where the ground is flat the path consists only of a cleared and weeded way to walk; where there is a significant slope, the stepping-stones highlight the changes in level and indicate a solid place to put your foot. My paths will win no prizes in the Garden Construction competitions, but they look real and they are functional. The carpet of cedar needles that covers them gives a rather nice brownish surface and a good springy feeling underfoot.

Then I trimmed back the blowsy old honeysuckles. These wild bush honeysuckles have a charming bloom in the spring, and some of mine are actually a good pink color rather than the usual white; otherwise I can't say much for them. Their habit of growth is best described as bizarre, with knots and angles that are very hard to sculpt into shape; the grayish, sinewy trunks and stems are unattractive in themselves; and the leaves are uninteresting in both shape and color. On the other hand, there they were, and I didn't at that time have anything to replace them with. So I did my best. The bayberries, in contrast, which grow only where there is a good amount of sun, are aesthetically highly satisfactory, having dark green glossy leaves and a branching system that lends itself to heavy pruning. You can leave a healthy, dense bayberry alone and it makes a wonderful solid mound, up to ten feet high; if it's sick or winter-damaged you can prune it so severely that it looks like something leaning over a cliff in a Japanese print. You can even cut it completely down, nearly to the ground, and in about three years you will have a brand-new healthy-looking bush. The birds like its clumps of gray berries.

I cleaned out all the brambles—a never-ending job, like that of cleaning out all the poison ivy; and I trimmed back the multiple clumps of arrowwood, which like the honeysuckle had grown to grotesque heights in an effort to reach the light. Arrowwood doesn't have a whole lot to recommend it, any more than honeysuckle does; but it was *something*, once it was reduced to the semblance of a shrub.

There was a blackberry bush growing in the moist soil at the very bottom of the hill, in close embrace with yet another overgrown honeysuckle. I thought a blackberry bush would be a lovely thing to have, and treated it very respectfully for about three years. But its arching fifteen-foot canes just took up too much room in all directions, so that you couldn't get through any of the paths without getting scratched. And the birds (of course) saw to it that we never got a single blackberry. In the end I gave up and dug it out.

A few sickly-looking poplar trees were adding nothing to the landscape, squeezing up uncomfortably among the cedars; they were sacrificed. But one rather mature wild cherry at the lower part of the Wild Garden had sent out long, nearly horizontal branches, stretching toward the sun. With a certain amount of pruning (for which I did have to get some professional help) this made a nice high, leafy canopy for the otherwise open stretch here, and the dark slanting trunks (wild cherries go in for multiple trunks on the slightest provocation)

56

make a good accent in the midst of light-green ferniness in the spring and summer.

In the course of this rather heavy labor I recognized the need for places to sit and rest, or plan, or contemplate. Accordingly, at the very lowest point of the gully, where I had found myself resting repeatedly with my back against a bank, I dug in a little and built a small stone loveseat (stones are always available here) with the help of a visiting college student. The next year, with the help of a different visitor and my daughter, I dug into the upper part of the hillside where Poison Ivy Plaza used to be and created a small sitting terrace. Here we had the amazing luck to uncover, right at the back of this space, two large rocks already in place, which with just a little tilting and bracing and supplementing formed a splendid if somewhat irregular bench against the dug-out bank. In a still later year my son built two wide curving stone steps to mark off and retain the lower end of the terrace, and all these stones promptly acquired delightful embellishments of moss and violets and bloodroot and ferns (I leave them while they're small and move them when they outgrow the spot). From here one sees, in comfort, the whole of the Wild Garden and the Gravel Pit.

Now I had the skeleton, or outline, of my Wild Garden. For the next two summers I made dozens of trips to the North Stonington dump and brought back mountain laurels, young dogwoods, half a dozen kinds of ferns, Solomon's seal and great merrybells and wild geranium (cranesbill) and jewelweed and jack-in-the-pulpit and wild celandine and native daylilies and starflowers. From the beach, well above high-water mark, I brought lots of wild blue flag, which makes a pleasant show in the spring, looking just wild enough to be thoroughly romantic. I planted clumps of lemon lilies (which combine extremely well with the blue flag) and bleeding hearts and lily of the valley

and Confederate violets—all from my mother's garden in Vermont—and added a few interrupted ferns that I found behind her grapevine, and some creeping Charlie that was infesting her lawn but that I saw as a fine ground cover for the woods (I was right). I sent away for more exotic ferns and for astilbes and trilliums and primroses and cardinal flower and fancy violets and bloodroot and Dutchman's breeches and foamflower. (I am mentioning here only those things that survived and spread and are, today, the major elements in the Wild Garden; I pass over with a silent tear the dozens of gorgeous wildflowers and ground covers that didn't like it and stayed only one or two seasons, if at all.)

I didn't, and still don't, find it necessary to do any significant overall "improving" of the soil in the Wild Garden, although some books will tell you that you must dig out the existing soil for at least eight inches and replace it with "woodsy soil" or "leafy compost." It seemed to me that soil that had been supporting the thick and varied growth I found initially was going to be adequate for anything I proposed to plant there, within reason.

To help new transplants from the wild to make a comfortable adjustment, I dug up each one with a goodly amount of its own native soil, disturbed as little as possible, and deposited the whole unit in a large planting hole liberally lined with compost and watered before and after planting. Plants that could not survive such a transfer were just too demanding for me; I made no further concessions to their temperament. This approach works in my particular garden, with a consistently high percentage of successful moves and a perfectly acceptable proportion of subsequent self-propagation—the ultimate indicator of a successful transplantation.

Forget-me-nots, raised from seed, were a tremendous success here; I had them on both sides of the major path on the west and in patches further back. They spread themselves around in the most engaging way and turned the whole area into a dream of pale blue in the spring. You will have noted that I use the past tense: suddenly, late one summer, all the forget-me-nots turned black and died, and the next year there was not one to be seen. I recall one other gardening book in which the same phenomenon is described but not explained; I assume it is caused by a viral blight of some kind. Now that ten or twelve years have gone by, it is reasonable to hope that a new planting would do well, but I haven't tried it yet.

Another success from seeds was the harebell, *Campanula rotundifolia*—alas, also temporary. For several years this fairylike creature populated the retaining wall of giant rocks that keeps the Gravel Pit from sliding down into the gully. It was never a very free seeder as the catalog said it would be, but it did spread some, to my great pleasure. Then something in the ecological balance struck it the wrong way and it died out over about three years. I tried moving some of the seedlings to the rock garden, but they survived only briefly.

The birds brought me a present here. One June day as I was resting on the stone loveseat in the gully, I was astonished to see three foxgloves in full bloom in the sunny part of the Wild Garden. Their offspring have been with us ever since, seeding themselves with great enthusiasm and often in highly pictur-esque and appropriate spots. I let them do pretty much what they want to because I like their architectural grace and their lovely variegated colors; when they show up where you don't want them, they're easy to pull up.

For quite a number of years I continued to experiment and add new things to the Wild Garden, and even to plan specific sequences of bloom with sophisticated color schemes, as if it were one extended, rambling perennial border. The planning was great fun, but most of these projects took an inordinate amount of special care and, even with care, either languished or looked too contrived. And I gradually realized that what one wants from a Wild Garden is an overall sense of peace and greenery, not a riot of colorful bloom. Then I relaxed and began to enjoy it, and to realize that I had already achieved pretty much what I had set out to, an agreeable area to walk to and around and back from, or even to sit in for a while, with some-thing of mild interest going on in all seasons. Where flowering plants have settled in comfortably, especially if they have ar-rived of their own volition, I make them extremely welcome. But I no longer feel the need to complement each kind of flower with two or three others, to make a "composition"; nor do vistas with no flowers, in this setting, strike me as lacking any essential beauty.

Today, ground covers from various sources have spread and met in a more or less continuous carpet, and my only problem is keeping them to some reasonable degree separated and out of the paths. A large part of the Wild Garden has Baltic ivy for its floor; this has the advantage that it climbs up the cedar trees that have lost their lower branches and clothes them in green, which adds a good deal to one's visual comfort. It has the disadvantage, however, that almost nothing can coexist with it, so I have to be alert as the green wave approaches other low plantings, and keep it well cut back.

Other large areas have vinca (periwinkle). These are mostly the places where daffodils bloom in spring, and the vinca, blooming (in periwinkle blue, naturally) at the same time, makes a wonderful background for the yellow clumps. During the rest of the year it provides a special note of dark-green crispness and vitality that nothing else quite achieves.

The creeping Charlie (I think this one is a *nummularia*) from my mother's lawn covers a large interior area, with here and there, on its edges, patches of foamflower (*Tiarella cordifolia*), which has its good years and its bad years. A long stretch of the lower path is thickly bordered with sweet woodruff, a beautiful sight in May when it breaks into multitudinous dainty white bloom (they say you can make May wine from this but I have not done so).

My mother's lily of the valley has its allotted areas (and no intention whatever of staying in them, but I am quite firm) in part sun, and in the deeper shade wild ginger has spread for yards and yards. This has glossy dark-green heart-shaped leaves and grows so thickly that it almost never has to be weeded. In the spring, each stem produces, well under the leaf and invisible unless you take the trouble to lift it up and look, a quaint little vase of a blossom that is apparently made out of dark-red velvet. Children like this.

A number of mosses have come in by themselves, filling in wherever there is no other ground cover. They are at their best in the cool moist winter months, and make the Wild Garden very beautiful in January, with or without snow. And there is something called pearlwort, a little more leafy than moss but still more mossy-looking than leafy-looking; what it really looks like is short, curly green hair. This came from seed, a bit against my expectations, and has established itself over considerable stretches of the relatively moist deep soil along the paths at the lowest level. In summer the various ferns also cover the ground or make structural statements throughout the Wild Garden; near the paths, and in artistic juxtaposition to some of the tall cedars, I have put Christmas ferns, which hold up nearly all winter and maintain the design of the garden when so much else has subsided.

Upon this floor, there are still a few honeysuckle bushes, which I have encouraged in places where they get enough sun to show a good bloom in the spring. All the bayberry has also been encouraged, as I consider it a most desirable shrub. But a good deal of the honeysuckle, and practically all of the messy and too-prolific arrowwood, has by now given place to mountain laurels and various small rhododendrons and a lovely wild shrub called sweet pepper bush that blooms in late summer with a most penetrating and delightful fragrance. Half a dozen dogwood trees came happily to maturity and gave me much joy for several years, but all succumbed to the anthracnose that is devastating all the dogwoods in this area, and whether it will be possible to replace them or whether, like American elms and chestnuts, they are about to become extinct for our lifetime, I don't yet know.

The Wild Garden, currently, gives a most convincing impression of being unplanned and unplanted. Its appeal is subtle and not, apparently, for everyone, though children relish its unassuming secretive charm and its twisting paths leading always to "another place in the forest." There must be something childish in me too, because when I ask myself, "Why am I spending all these hours weeding and trimming this place?"—it has to be thoroughly groomed twice a year or it reverts to jungle—I come up, and repeatedly, with the answer that I simply like to be there, and I like to take care of it because that is my excuse for being there.

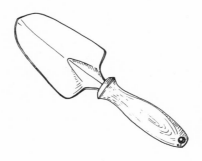

Propagating Plants

About two years after I began gardening in a serious way, I became the lucky tenant of a penthouse apartment in New York City that had a large open terrace and, in one corner, a small greenhouse. For a considerable period, just at that crucial time, I was able to raise quite a lot of plants from seed and cuttings, thanks to this ideal environment, and bring them to the country for transplanting to the outdoors only when they had become thrifty little plants.

This was extremely important to my young garden. Neither sowing directly on the ground nor trying to raise things from seed in a south window in the country house worked for me because I never seemed to be there to supply moisture at the crucial moment. And, of all the things I tried to raise "on site" from broadcast or even properly sown and bedded seed, I recall successes only with nemophila one summer (never again), with creeping thyme, and with Dutchman's breeches, which was the only thing that showed itself from two whole packets of "wild-flower seeds." Eventually I decided those were flukes, and stopped trying the outdoor method. But things that I could nurse along in the greenhouse until they reached a size for independent living turned out very well, and furnished a majority of my early plantings aside from those I scavenged from the neighboring territories.

Forget-me-nots, as I said in the last chapter, were an early and spectacular success until they were swept away by some natural disaster; harebells (English bluebells) were another. Both arabis and alyssum came up readily from seed, as did the perennial candytuft; all have become permanent residents of my secret garden in the Gravel Pit. Columbines of all kinds, and pinks of all kinds, have been very easy to raise from seed. But I never had any luck with the more exotic kinds of rock-garden plants, nor with most of the gray-leaved little creatures that live naturally in dry soil; there seems to be, for these, a most delicate balance between the moisture they need in order to thrive and that which is too unlike their desert homes. Sometimes they were affected by damping-off, a disease caused by soil fungi and resulting in rot in the stem of the just-emerged little plant so that it topples over and dies. I was, probably irrationally, against using chemical treatment to prevent this. Very likely sterilized potting soil would have been better than the sifted compost I used, but even that smacked too much of technology for my taste. Once, in a frenzy of enthusiasm after reading a particularly persuasive author, I sterilized some compost in my oven. Once only; it was a smell never to be forgotten, and the experiment ruined all my cookie sheets.

As time went by a number of things changed. I was now in a position to buy whole flats of little plants if I wanted something new; and if they weren't always the particular variety that some book had raved about, my experience was that "particular varieties" tended to be finicky and short-lived in my garden, whereas the sturdy standbys grown and offered by the local nursery stood up to my kind of treatment and gave just as good an overall effect. Better: dead and sickly plants, however "special" in theory, fail of their primary purpose in a garden meant for general enjoyment.

Then, after a number of years in which I laboriously raised things like foxgloves and black-eyed Susans and bleeding heart from seed and even ferns from spores—which was a thrill—I began to realize that these plants were cheerfully seeding *themselves*, all over my property, in ideal places for them to grow, and I could either leave them right there or wait until they were big enough to be moved. My painstaking artificial methods, while the source of a good deal of ego gratification, were totally unnecessary for a majority of the plants I was interested in— namely, plants that *would* thrive and reproduce themselves naturally under the conditions obtaining in my garden. I also became tired, at last, of the very high failure rate of my attempts to raise more exotic and "interesting" plants, and decided that those grapes were sour.

But the decisive reason for the discontinuance of my seed-raising efforts was that the Buildings Department of the City of New York came around one day and inspected my greenhouse (which had been there twenty years before we ever moved in) and said it had been built originally without a permit and it was therefore not to be permitted. We protested most movingly over a period of several months, but to no avail; the greenhouse was dismantled and that was the end of my career as a seedswoman. It was fun while it lasted.

I also experimented with a variety of other methods of propagation. The first is so primitive and obvious it hardly deserves the fancy name "vegetative propagation"; it consists of the simple division of large clumps of a given plant into multiple small clumps, each with a proportionate amount of root, which are then planted independently (the usually deteriorated center of the old clump being often discarded). That is something anybody can do, and I don't think I've ever failed with it as long as there was enough good root on each new section. According to the books, you should do this every two or three years to "keep your perennials in good condition." Well, I don't know. If by good condition is meant continuously and vigorously expanding, maybe. But my astilbes and irises and daylilies and hostas and coralbells seem to stay perfectly healthy and bloom without any diminution that I can see for years and years. Basically I only divide them when I want more of them or when they crowd their neighbors; for my kind of garden, that seems to be quite adequate. I *have* learned that if you are starting off with just a few plants of one kind, or just one, and you want to propagate them to the utmost so as to make yourself a whole little colony, it pays to give them extra good, extra deep soil and treat them nicely in relation to water and fertilizer; these things do make a difference. But normally I don't want things to grow so fast.

I have successfully propagated by "layering," too. Starting with one little lilac shoot scavenged from an abandoned farm in the first year we had this place, I now have four blooming bushes, the three offspring having been produced in the approved way by cutting partway into a low branch, wedging the cut open with a twig, bending it down to ground level and burying it a couple of inches in a nice nourishing microenvironment of pure compost, with a heavy stone on top to prevent its drying out or springing up. You then wait a couple of years and one fine spring day you dig it up and find that the wounded branch has grown itself a lovely clutch of roots, whereupon you sever its connection with its parent and plant it wherever you want your new lilac bush. This is undeniably a bit slow, but it's cheap, easy, and foolproof.

I also use layering to help along the spread of new ground covers like creeping juniper and vinca—any ground cover, really. You take a peripheral frond (which will spontaneously root where it touches the ground, eventually; but you want to speed things up), make a cut into its underside about five inches back from the tip and wedge it open, make a miniature bed of good composty soil under this cut and cover it with another inch or so of more soil held firmly down by a good-sized stone, and there you are. You do this all around the circumference of your plant and, for extra encouragement, keep it well watered, and presently it "attaches" with new roots and starts expanding with correspondingly increased vigor. (In this method, you don't detach the newly rooted tip, because what you want is an enlargement of your existing planting.)

The above is the correct way to do it. However, for ground covers that are less woody and are going to expand quite fast anyway, all you need to do is to toss a little moist soil or compost near the periphery of the planting and water it now and then, eliminating the rigmarole with the cut and the wedge and the stone. Any ground cover worthy of its name *wants* to cover the ground, and soon enough your problem will be in restraining it rather than encouraging it.

In the extreme case of things like sedums, an excellent system is to lay one small piece of the plant on the surface of the soil and go away. To keep this ground cover thoroughly healthy, come around once or twice a year and remove every morsel of it that you can see, carefully digging up all the roots as well. You may think I exaggerate, but the solemn fact is that I have yet to eliminate any sedum from a spot where it has been once established. You can, with perseverance, keep it under some kind of control, but elimination is not a feasible goal. It seeds and spreads to other areas, too.

I have found roses quite amenable to stem cuttings, a process whereby you cut off a few inches of the current year's growth toward the end of the summer, insert the cut end in moist sand, cover the whole thing with a plastic bag to prevent too much loss of water from the leaves (but the bag should have some air holes so your plant doesn't get steamed on a hot day), and wait for several months, at the end of which time your cutting has produced a healthy ball of roots and it's spring and you plant it out in your garden feeling very pleased with yourself. My successes with this method were all in the greenhouse, and were with roses only; I never could get azaleas or pussywillows or sweet pepper bush to make roots, either inside or (as the books said was possible) in a seed frame left outdoors in a sheltered place, or even in a cold frame.

The cold frame is a story in itself, but a short, sad one. My father made it for me according to the best specifications, and I tried it both in a sunny spot and in a semi-shady spot. The problem resulted from my only being here weekends: if I left the glass top open the little seedlings dried up, and if I left it almost closed and the sun came out, the temperature would rise immediately and everything would cook. In the end I decided that a cold frame is like a cradle; it's a convenient piece of equipment but in no way takes the place of a mother who is there when you need her.

When it comes to creating a sizable area of ground cover in a new place, I can report an interesting if inadvertent experiment. At one side of our house, screening it from the driveway, is a group of about eight mature cedar trees. We had added some at each end to expand the planting, but weren't happy with the condition of the grass under them, which had a distinctly starved and suffocated look and got very little light. In addition, the tree trunks were suffering increasingly from being knocked and sliced by the monster lawn mowers that lawn people have taken to using these days, which are not really very appropriate for small irregular lawn areas like ours.

So one summer, when both my son and my son-in-law were in residence and asked if they could "do anything," I took unfair advantage of their goodness and asked them to dig up the grass sod under and around the cedars (a total area of approximately three hundred square feet), take it to the compost pile, and bring back and mix in six inches of compost so I could establish a ground cover. They were charmingly willing, but both the charm and the willingness declined perceptibly as the August afternoons wore on.

By the beginning of the third day, with the job only half done, it was apparent that I had exceeded the bounds of a reasonable request; and in order to get it somehow finished I said, All right, for the other half leave the grass there, just put a six-inch layer of compost on top. This they did in about two hours flat, and I planted the whole area the same evening by the simple method of pulling up pieces of rooted pachysandra from a nearby area and pushing them into the compost about eight inches apart, with a thorough watering afterward and subsequent waterings twice a week all through the fall.

71

The instructive result of this experience was that there was no discernible difference in the "take" or the progress of the plantings between the half that was properly dug and the half that just had compost tossed onto it. Specifically, no grass penetrated the thick layer of compost from below; apparently the sod that was left in place simply rotted and allowed the pachysandra roots to grow into it as freely as in the other half. (On both halves, wildflowers came up in profusion from all that compost. The first spring, when the pachysandra coverage was still rather thin, I left them there and they made a pretty little show under the trees—foxgloves and columbines and blue flag and buttercups and pinks; later that summer I removed them to the Wild Garden.) I weeded the area twice during the second summer, and since then it, like my other pachysandra plantings, has needed only the briefest of cleanups each spring.

For extensive coverage with ivy or cotoneaster—which are a little slower to establish but perfectly frightening in their zeal once they have their roots well into the ground—I have made individual small planting holes, about twelve inches apart, six inches deep and four in diameter, filled them with compost, and inserted rooted cuttings. In the case of these plants, cuttings are easily obtained: any long stem of the plant that has been in contact with the soil can be gently teased up and will be found to have made little clusters of roots every few inches. You cut the stem into sections, each section having a cluster of roots and a couple of short side branches aboveground. These sections are "rooted cuttings" (of one kind), and as long as the proportion of root to leaf is adequate, each section will now function as an independent young plant. Watering and weeding have to be carefully attended to for a good two years; then, just as you decide the whole project was a bad idea and something must be wrong with your soil, you come out one day and find you have a solid, flourishing ground cover. From that point on, no special care is necessary. No weeds can penetrate, no drought discourage. All your attention can now be devoted to keeping your infant Hercules (no longer an infant) within bounds.

The Rock Garden
and How It Grew

To the north, where the house was dug deeply into the rocky hillside, there was a steep bank amounting almost to a cliff, and as bare as the Gravel Pit to begin with. On its summit was a good big spread of wild blueberries, and one elderly wild cherry tree just overhung the raw edge. This part of our property seems to consist very largely of a kind of granite scree, left behind by the retreating glacier; the soil is scanty and sandy, and you can't dig out even one spadeful of it without coming upon a rock the size of a football. It was that nearly vertical bank, cut into obviously inhospitable soil, that first gave me the idea of a rock garden.

At that early stage, my notion of a rock garden was similar

in overall concept to that of an afghan made of brightly colored granny squares: a more or less uniform surface, more or less uniformly studded with more or less uniform hunks of stone, alternating with more or less uniform clumps of color. But the Westerly Library (my wonderful and never-failing source of garden information) quickly educated me out of such naïveté. The principles of asymmetry and three-dimensionality were said to apply above all to rock gardens; they should resemble, or at least allow the imagination to project into them, romantic miniature landscapes. These ideas I found very stimulating, but the notion of producing such an effect on a bank as steep as mine, facing indeed south but shaded all day by the house itself, was too much for me.

I had by this time discovered Hall's honeysuckle, a ubiquitous trailing and twining weed in these parts, and managed via my New York City greenhouse to create a dozen or so thriving plants from roadside cuttings. I spotted them around the bank, and they flourished mightily but—as I might have realized in advance had I thought about it—they never bloomed worth speaking of because of not getting any sun. Hall's honeysuckle has a wonderful foamy look and infinitely satisfying fragrance when in bloom, and almost no other desirable characteristics; but it was several years before I found this out, and then I was busy with other things, and after a while we dug up that whole bank and built an addition to the house where it used to be so the problem was solved.

Meanwhile I had developed an appetite for a rock garden, and presently one was vouchsafed to me.

I've mentioned the paths I'd made through the blueberry patch at the back (north) of the house, purely for practical purposes. You reached this area from the east side of the house, where the front door was, by another path that led past two enormous half-submerged rocks looking for all the world like a couple of bathing hippos. One weekend early in our third year I cleaned out messy places along this path, including a considerable growth of wild raspberries and a real thicket of poison ivy, and found that I had thus created a lovely little irregular clearing measuring about fifteen by twenty feet. You approached this clearing by a meandering ascent around a clump of young arrowwood, bounded by blueberry bushes on most sides, attractively furnished already with a number of good weathered lichen-covered rocks and two small wild cherry trees but mostly in full sun.

Here was, undoubtedly, the place for my rock garden, and I began it that same weekend, moving (with the help of my daughter and her strong young college friends) other rocks into more picturesque groupings and working valiantly away at the nearly solid tangle of roots composing the "soil." (It was while pulling at all those roots, after moving all those rocks, that I became disagreeably aware of a structure I had always taken for granted, namely My Back. That is a story in itself but it doesn't belong in this book, so let me dispose of it by saying that more than twenty years later I'm still gardening with the same enthusiasm and pretty much the same vigor; only I do exercises every day, and my planning in relation to garden work routinely includes a preliminary conference with My Back to obtain its advice and consent.)

This was the Rock Garden of our first ten years here: just a widening of the path that led north from the house out toward the golf course. You came upon it unexpectedly around a bend in the path that skirted some blueberry bushes, and it spread itself before you quite appetizingly, I thought, reaching its climax under the wild cherry tree at the top of the rise. It was hidden from the house the way a rock garden is supposed to be, and was altogether quite a miniature little place, with a wild and neglected charm, especially when the lemon lilies from my mother's garden and the wild blue flag from the beach were in bloom.

But then we made a sizable addition to the north side of the house, nearly doubling our interior space; and a good thing too, since by now there were sons-in-law and a daughter-in-law and a couple of granddaughters, all of whom seemed to think Woodwinds was a fine place to spend their summer vacation. The bank with the honeysuckle disappeared and so did the wild cherry that crowned it and the southern part of the blueberry patch. One of the hippos was blown up and carted away.

The back of the house (toward the north) now became the front of the house, with a stone terrace twelve feet wide along its whole facade. The terrace ended in an eighteen-inch stone wall that enclosed it completely and separated it from the Rock Garden. The stepping-stone path that led so charmingly up to the Rock Garden was replaced by a wide, curved stone staircase that was now our formal entrance (not that anyone ever uses it as such); this was flanked by furry grayish junipers, with a Korean dogwood in the middle of one side and a shadbush in the middle of the other side.

Now the problem was that the house and the Rock Garden were tête-à-tête, separated only by the terrace, and the Rock Garden only extended over about half the width of the house. Clearly it had to be enlarged to some degree of symmetry, and equally clearly it had to be civilized a little bit. So the surrounding blueberries were pushed back a few more feet, and a whole new section to the Rock Garden was created, about fifteen feet in diameter.

In the-off center of this area an arrangement of rocks was placed, and around them went expanded new plantings; around this went an irregular circle of stepping-stones (thanks to my good husband), and around the stepping-stones a border of more plantings. The Rock Garden was now a kind of visual extension of the terrace, and agreeable to saunter around if anyone felt like getting up from his comfortable chair under the umbrella for five minutes. (People actually do that once in a while; the Rock Garden plants are still best seen up close.)

It seemed to me that this area had now acquired a more formal status altogether, and should be dignified and accented by something in the architectural way; and after consideration I installed a plain concrete birdbath just off center in the new section and arranged a tiny pipe to drip water into it. The pipe comes out from the house underground (thanks to a strong and helpful son-in-law) in the form of a plastic tube and ends in a copper tip that curls over the top of a cleverly placed rock, leaning over the birdbath and dripping sweetly into it. This all looked somewhat raw and peculiar at first, but both the copper piping and the concrete of the birdbath darkened presently into a nice mottled brown, and the euonymus I moved from a place where it had sulked for four years took hold (with the boost from all that water, I suppose) and concealed the plumbing successfully, and now the whole arrangement is to my mind convincingly evocative of a real mountain freshet issuing spontaneously from a real, wild, fantastic cliff and falling (for all of eight inches) into a real mountain tarn. Eight inches is plenty to create the essential splash, I found; splash is important both to soothe the mind, which it does, and to attract the birds, which it also—definitely—does. In the heat of a summer day they line up as many as ten or twelve at a time and the rate of dripping has to be increased substantially to keep up with their ablutions.

To contemplate this picture of rustic charm I acquired a little Saint Francis (also made of concrete) and stood him across the path, about seven feet away, surrounded by miniature shrubs and with his back to another good big rock. He looks, I fondly think, as if he has just come out of the woods after a climb, and discovered this little dell ahead of him, and is pausing to have holy thoughts on the subject of refreshment. In the winter, in the snow, I imagine that he is rapt in meditation on the turn of the year and the mutability of all that lives; these being very much my own meditations at that time, I find him good company when I glance out the window in the darkening day.

I have tried to grow, in this little bit of ground, almost everything they talk about for rock gardens. I began by planting things I'd read about in the rock garden books, and lovely little creatures they are, by name and description: *Dryas octopetala, Aquilegia flabellata nana, Polemonium reptans, Saponaria ocymoides.* I used to make diagrams of how I'd plant them and how they'd look (in three dimensions), and I can remember lying awake at night just running the exotic beautiful names over my mind's tongue. I bought seeds and ordered plants of nearly every rock garden variety I saw advertised (it's true I never worked from specialized rock garden catalogs, only from generalists). And I learned things.

I learned that rock garden plants, like garden plants in general, are not all that easy to grow, and that the catalogs, and even the books, don't tell you that. They describe what a given plant will do under favorable conditions, with professional-level care, but seldom warn you that without such conditions and such care you are doomed to failure. Some of the more considerate authors go so far as to tell you whether a particular plant likes sun or shade, acid or alkaline soil; a few zealous souls even give separate cookbook-type recipes for special soils for special plants. It seems you are supposed to create little stony pockets for these delicate ones and keep them in their own micro-mini-environment, presumably replenishing with an eyedropper week by week the nutrients they have condescended to use up. Needless to say, anything with that kind of requirement never got tried out in *my* rock garden; I stuck for the most part to things that were described as "rampant" or "invasive," or that were said to "multiply freely from seed."

Only for me they didn't. I found myself following, in my rock-garden career, the experience of many years in relation to African violets indoors. The plants just died. The seedlings sometimes came along pretty well in the greenhouse, but as soon as I planted them out they moped and fussed and said they didn't like it there and, after producing a few pathetic blossoms in the first season, quietly failed to show up the next.

The trouble, I finally realized, was that I didn't really have a proper rock-garden environment. Most successful rock gardeners live in areas where water supply is not a problem and temperatures are not extreme. England, for example, or the state of Washington. Naturally occurring rock gardens are found on high mountain screes; they *look* barren and bony just like my land, but they are fed by melting snow and during their growing season they are never at a loss for moisture. I also realized that after they finish growing and blooming most of them simply dry up and disappear until the next year; very sensible of them, but not just the thing in a garden intended for viewing at all seasons.

Now, in Watch Hill there is a kind of rainy season in April and May, when you can't stay ahead of the weeds even if you work at it all your waking hours; you can't keep your perennials pinched and staked; and the bittersweet you cut down on Sunday is back by the following Friday. But during July and August, there is essentially *no* rain—only a heavy morning mist from the sea and frequent thundershowers that roll off the dust and down the hill without any idea of doing any good to the plant life. During this period a public dictum is sent forth rather frequently that sprinkling of lawns and gardens is not allowed; you can carry pailfuls of water (to the limits set by your back), or rely, I suppose, on water piped underground to your precious plant materials; or you can sit there and watch them wither.

Or, of course, you can create a garden that is a combination of rock garden and desert garden, inhabited not by wide green fronds but by tough spiny gray things that hoard their water as fiercely as cactuses. And the older I get the more I have tended toward this kind of garden, which on the whole is more satisfactory more of the time, and *never* requires pailfuls of water to be carried to it. (Actually I do, in dry weather, water it quite generously with the slow-drip hose once a week, with the idea of soaking the soil deep enough to seduce the little roots into growing down to their maximum length, thus being less vulnerable when the next dry period comes and the top three or four inches have turned to powder.) This approach seems to be working pretty well and gives me a nice blooming garden all year long, with a minimum of exertion.

The first growing thing that showed any interest in settling down in my rock garden was a creeping thyme that I grew from seed. Not the same creeping thyme I had in the Gravel Pit; this one was *Thymus minimus*, reaching all of an inch high in full bloom on moist soil. Over most of the Rock Garden it appears as a mat not more than a quarter of an inch deep, which is rather nice because it shows all the attractive irregularities of the terrain, just clothing it in a rich dark-green mantle.

A couple of years after I started this, I got a lovely white cousin from a wildflower nursery; they called it "White Mountain Thyme" (I've never been sure whether this name implies a white thyme from the mountains or a thyme from the White Mountains.) It is identical to the *minimus* except for being just a bit lighter green and having white blooms instead of purple. I had only one container of it, but it spread most obligingly, and within three years I was able to intersperse these two over the whole area of the Rock Garden, filling in between the stepping-stones and making a lovely carpet wherever there is nothing else. In bloom, which happens at the same time as the late daffodils—and the violets—the whole garden is, briefly, the prettiest mosaic of shades of white, yellow, and purple that can be imagined. And all the rest of the year the thyme keeps the place looking somehow decent and thriving, even when nothing particular is going on.

Other largish areas of the Rock Garden are clothed in "mountain pink" (*Phlox subulata*), in pale blue, white, and pink. This comes into bloom in the spring along with various small narcissi and makes a pretty picture of fresh pastels. The books talk about how rampageously this stuff spreads; all I can say is, in *my* garden it doesn't, nor does it seed itself at all intrusively. It just sits there looking civilized and comfortable all year long, and for the entire month of May it is quite heavenly.

Thrift, or *Armeria maritima*, is one of numerous experimental plants I bought in single three-inch pots from an open-air nursery in the middle of the Wall Street area of New York City. (I used to resort to this place on my lunch hour, and think gardening thoughts, and then go back to work refreshed with some small new treasure in a paper bag.) It has done well wherever I put it, and it has finally spread, in the Rock Garden, to a respectable patch about six feet square that looks green and— well—thrifty all year round. Its blooms are small shaggy lollipops of bright pink, which hold up for several weeks in the late spring. Again, the books warn you sternly about how thrift will die out in the center and need dividing and replanting fairly frequently; mine has maintained itself without attention for seven years now. It seems there are real advantages to keeping one's garden a bit on the starved side, just as with houseplants that you don't want to outgrow their space too fast.

At each end of the long axis of the Rock Garden is a little froth of *Geranium lancastriense* (Wargrave Pink), which blossoms all summer long and whose leaves are decorative in themselves. These plants do appreciate a rich moist soil and a little fertilizer, so I give it to them because they repay the attention. They get heavily mulched with compost in April and November, and a mouthful or two of bone meal in mid-July. They are, in fact, somewhat spoiled little creatures by my standards; I suppose every mother has her favorites.

For dignity and (relative) height I have a number of good small shrubs. But not all of them want to be good and stay small. For example, I planted a dwarf yew once, from the local nursery, smack in the middle of the Rock Garden. It made a splendid focal point and was a lovely dark green. For several years it behaved itself nicely and then its roots apparently found their way down into some Aladdin's Cave of unimaginable richness and it began to grow at the rate of twelve to eighteen inches a year, in all directions. In vain I lopped off great armfuls for Christmas decorations (they are wonderful in the house, lasting a good three weeks without water and without shedding), and every spring rescued the little delicate plants cowering in its shade. But its shade got to be eight feet in diameter. Ten feet. This is a *dwarf* yew? Half the Rock Garden was hidden to view from the living room windows. Finally I faced the fact that this was no shrub for a miniature garden, and had it removed to a place on the edge of the property where it nicely faces down a group of hemlocks. In its heyday, this yew actually produced two offspring, all the way across the parking area; at least, I don't know where else those new yews could have sprung from. Fortunately, they are in a good location.

Another shrub that serves as a focal point is in the center of the plantings that surround the birdbath. It, too, is a "dwarf" and it, too, is somewhat overgrown, but not yet ready for banishment. It's a Japanese spirea, bought from a mail order catalog, and as satisfactory a little bush as you could ask for, with a perfect shower of pink-and-white posies in early July, and some repeating later on. It's not evergreen, but being surrounded by hummocks of thyme and heath which *are* evergreen, it serves to give a nice variety of texture in the winter months.

There is a low-growing evergreen shrub that looks a bit— only a bit—like a creeping yew. Its name is *Pachistima canbyi*; it has no common name. I forget where I acquired my one original specimen; it must have been a particularly vigorous one, because even in the thin rock-garden soil it has spread around and under a whole central complex of rocks in the most satisfying way, looking extremely at home and healthy. However, my joy in this phenomenon (one of my earlier success stories) began to be mitigated when little shoots of pachistima started showing up in the middle of my stepping-stone path, and in neighboring rock groups, and in amongst plantings of other things. In short, it spreads by underground roots; these are yellow and incredibly tough and run a good three to four inches under the surface. Once pachistima has invaded another planting it's a question of digging the whole area up to eradicate the roots, and then replacing your desired plants. Of course you have in this process improved the soil of the area and the pachistima promptly reinvades. I've tried painting the little shoots with undiluted herbicide and I've tried just persistently and repeatedly pulling off the top growth wherever it appears unwanted. But nothing discourages them for long, and I'm about ready to call it quits with this plant; which is too bad, because in its proper place it really is a most attractive little six-inch-high clamberer. I have occasionally seen pachistima described in gardening books and nobody else seems to have my problems with it; I may have just got hold of an exceptionally rambunctious version.

More and more I have fallen in love with the tribe of heaths and heathers. This affection started with a single plant of *Erica carnea* that performed valiantly for fifteen years on the West Bank, blooming from November through March in an unlikely shade of pinkish mauve. It encouraged me to expand, and by now I have half a dozen little evergreen mounds scattered around the Rock Garden. They spread slowly but handsomely, they are highly resistant to infiltration by weeds, they bloom in various colors at various seasons, and they have, to my mind, a certain compact elegance. The bloom lasts from one to two months, but there is a whole month beforehand when the little spires of colorful buds are quite charming, and the architecture of the faded blooms is still attractive. There is one drawback about heaths in this particular climate, though; they do occasionally die off in a severe winter. I have consistently lost new plantings made in the fall, even as early as October; now I only plant in the spring. And even the mature plants suffer when it is very cold. However, I don't protect them. To me, a winter garden covered with evergreen boughs or pieces of burlap is not a garden at all, it's a storage space; and who wants to look at a storage space out of the living room window? If one of my heaths dies (it doesn't happen very often), I replace it with one said to be extra hardy.

Now in addition to these wonderfully reliable mats and shrubs, which provide the framework of the Rock Garden and give it a definitive character all year round, I have a goodly variety of small colorful accent plants and groups of plants that set up their little tableaux here and there—sometimes a few at a time and sometimes whole companies at once—and transform the appearance of the garden from one season to the next. In the spring there are crocuses, and tiny species tulips and irises and daffodils. There is alyssum (the pale yellow kind), which makes a beautiful sunny show for an entire month in the spring, surrounded by Johnny-jump-ups; there are red coralbells and a small thicket of evergreen candytuft and more violets than I really want. Lilyturf, germander, and several kinds of dianthus—one from a seed packet, two scrounged from the wild—have all settled into flourishing little colonies. (Dianthus in all its forms, according to the books, is a lime-lover; my soil, throughout, is excruciatingly acid; yet dianthus seems to like my place. There is more to these matters than we know about.) Other wildflowers from the neighboring fields that have made themselves at home are the blue-eyed grass *Sisyrinchium mucronatum* which has one quick burst of bloom in July; the stiff-leaved aster *A. linariifolius* which keeps the garden "alive" all through October; and the yellow-eyed star grass *Hypoxis hirsuta* which goes full tilt from mid-May until frost.

In and amongst everything else, pulling the various clumps together, are sedums of various kinds: my faithful pink bloomer, an offspring from the Gravel Pit; *Sedum kamschaticum* with a golden flower; *Sedum erectum,* which has gray leaves and is self-respecting and reliable; and a tiny one whose name I don't know but call *Sedum minimus,* which mixes in with the ground-hugging thymes and adds its yellow bloom to their purple and white. There is also some hens-and-chickens (a sempervivum, not a sedum), which is good for filling in cracks between rocks. Mine rarely blooms, and when it does the foot-high flower stem covered with irregular scales has an ungainly dinosaurish look and I usually cut it off.

Under the blueberry bushes to the west of the Rock Garden, bordering the path that leads to the compost pile, are two adorable wildflowers that were here when I came; they have flourished charmingly but have resisted all efforts to establish them in more effective surroundings. On the right of the path is *Anemone quinquefolia*, the wood anemone, with a very pretty fancy leaf and a simple five-part white flower. On the left is a thick band of thyme-leaved sandwort, *Arenaria serpyllifolia*, with leaves that look much like chickweed but without chickweed's terrible proclivity for seeding, and with a much prettier flower, tiny and white and profuse and lasting for several weeks in early summer. I don't know what it is these two little nymphs like about the edge of the blueberry plantation, but they look fine there and have consistently refused transplantation, so I've decided that is just where they belong.

My rock garden is framed with daylilies, which provide color during July when the bulbs are totally gone and the small spring bloomers have had their say. I started with alternating plants of Hyperion (clear yellow) and Evelyn Claar (pink with a bit of salmon), just because I didn't have enough of either one to do the whole job. This made a somewhat garish show in the hot days of high summer, when simplicity and coolness are all you're looking for. So after a few years, when everything had doubled itself, I weeded out the Evelyn Claars and installed them in a new planting of their own, under the south deck, where they loom poetically out of the gloom.

Finally, at the western end of the terrace wall there stands like a graceful sentinel a white lilac bush that I scavenged from a large abandoned planting just off Route 2. It was planted in the original Rock Garden near its edge, and miraculously survived the construction of the terrace after being given up for lost, coming up moreover in a location that couldn't be improved on. I am keeping it small; it adds a certain stability to the terrace planting and its white, very fragrant blossoms make a splendid complement to the colorful carpet on the ground in May.

I am still calling this area the Rock Garden, but I'm not at all sure it hasn't evolved itself right out of that category over the years; by any name it is a pleasing place. The plants, as I have indicated, are mostly of the stubbly, bristly persuasion and their blossoms are small and unpretentious; their appeal is modest (except for one grand splash in midsummer), but real. Like most of my other "places," this one gives no particular sign of having been designed; it seems to have grown up around the rocks by itself. Personally I like the effect.

At present—it took a long time—the little plantings are mature; that is, the garden is fully clothed in "greenery" (ranging all the way from gray to reddish-brown) and needs only maintenance care. That includes endless laborious weeding-up of grasses from amongst the thyme, and twice-a-year rooting out of the encroaching blueberry bushes. I suppose if I installed a six-inch vertical barrier in the soil, made of metal or plastic, it would get rid of the root problem. But I can't bring myself to do that. For one thing, it seems like an enormous project of work all at once, and for another I really like the slow regular creep around this garden, twice a season, that brings me in close touch with its inner life and gives me a feel for its individual reality. This perception of work as pleasurable that others might experience as intolerably tedious is, I suspect, one basic reason why some of us are gardeners and some are not.

The Terrace

The terrace that was built between the "new" front of our house and the Rock Garden is made of Connecticut fieldstone in pleasantly variegated shades of gray and tan. We left about two feet of unpaved surface next to the house wall for a planting space; it was my plan to put junipers in there for architectural accents, and in fact I did that: low ones in the center, under the windows, and columnar shapes for the two corners of the house. I put in plenty of compost to get them off to a good start, and when the junipers arrived in midsummer— nice healthy young plants they were—I planted them carefully and tended them lovingly. Within nine months they were all dead: one of the mysteries by which my gardening is so remarkably plagued. This particular disaster may be charged to whatever toxic influence emanates from the house itself, which I have never investigated in a sensible analytic way—or it may be that these new junipers were susceptible to the same blight that has killed others in the area. Whatever the lethal agent, it was quick and thorough.

There didn't seem much point in planting the same kind of thing again, so I changed tactics and put in my mother's evening primroses for summer color, with a good backing of Christmas ferns for winter dignity. This has worked very well, and with these plants there have been no signs of any ill effects from the soil. The evening primroses—which I pinch back once or twice, otherwise they tend to get top-heavy and prostrate themselves over the terrace—are in full bloom all through July, but by mid-August the whole planting has reverted to a soothing dark green. In the last couple of years a family of foxgloves has arrived in their peripatetic way; in late summer I pull out all except a few toward the back, and these are quite pretty in June, when the violets and creeping Charlie that came in with the Christmas ferns are also in bloom.

Between the flat stones of the terrace floor I started a few clumps of *Thymus minimus*, which has spread to cover nearly half the surface; I have, in fact, begun to cut back its growth here and there so that some of the stonework continues to show. In the corners and along the edges of the wall violets, primroses, wild pinks, and Johnny-jump-ups have neatly seeded themselves and make a mild, agreeable decoration all through the summer. For the first two or three years I had geraniums in tubs in the corners of the terrace, but they were a bit intense, I decided, especially when the yellow and pink daylilies were in bloom too. The casual delicate tracery of the self-seeded wildflowers is quite sufficiently stimulating for the people who come to this terrace on hot afternoons, most of whom want only to put their feet up and let their minds drift free.

Along the outside of the terrace wall to the west I put Japanese quince. This was originally one plant from a mail order house that had been moved from place to place without ever finding a proper home. By the time the terrace was built it was probably eight years old, and readily divided into multiple sections. It makes a delightful hedge along the wall, and blooms madly in May, its vertical branches totally hidden by profuse double pink blossoms, with the violets at its feet (that I *cannot* eliminate) adding to the picture. I haven't fed it at all. When the soil begins to look thin and depleted, I add a couple of inches of compost, but this is an infrequent event; it seems to be an undemanding little shrub. My only complaint, in fact, about the Japanese quince is that after blooming it dies back for ten inches or so. This doesn't seem to keep it from being perfectly healthy otherwise, but it's a nuisance to have to prune all those individual tips (I don't believe in shearing such things off flat). Quite often I simply ignore it; within six weeks or so the new growth has overtaken the old dead stems and it's all right, but my conscience is unassuaged.

To the north, the terrace wall constitutes one side of the enclosure for the Rock Garden. This wall is planted sparsely with a very sweet-smelling blue German iris that came from my mother's garden—just to give a little color early in the summer—and thickly with daylilies, which I've described in connection with the Rock Garden. More of the same daylilies in irregular clumps along the western and northern edges of the Rock Garden echo this planting and demarcate the Rock Garden from its surrounding blueberry bushes, so that (it is my intention and belief) the daylilies provide an important transitional function, being sufficiently gardenlike in character to line the stone wall on the one hand, but sufficiently wild-looking to border the blueberries on the other.

Daylilies have one substantial flaw when they are placed for close and prolonged viewing: unless *all* the faded blooms are removed *every* morning, they hang on the stalk like old banana skins and spoil the fresh effect of the current day's crop. This irritation is enough to ruin a quiet sit-down in the presence of an ungroomed display of daylilies for anyone with the smallest propensity for "tidying up" in their nature. I wish the plantsmen would look into this and develop a daylily whose spent blooms detach themselves promptly and neatly.

The east terrace wall is much higher on the outside than on the terrace side, since the ground slopes steeply downward in this direction. It is clothed with ivy interwoven with a pretty and fragrant honeysuckle vine, Graham Thomas, that blooms off and on all summer, perfuming the sitting area and making nice little posies to put in visitors' bedrooms.

The stairs that curve down from terrace level to parking-area level are bordered by bits of hillside that we at first planted entirely to a low juniper, the same as we had on the West Bank. Alas for the futility of mortal endeavor, this juniper had no sooner covered the ground than it succumbed to blight. Strangely enough, the plants on one side of the steps died off completely but the other side (the one that continues on into the blueberries on the north) has been, so far, only minimally affected. This has presented a serious landscaping problem: as a Vermont Yankee born and bred, I simply cannot pull up so many healthy plants (the nurseryman tells me they will probably go eventually, but it's been three years now and I see no sign

of further deterioration), and yet it really does look a little strange to have junipers only on *one* side of the stairway.

In this dilemma, and without feeling that it was a very satisfactory solution, I have planted the "dead" side to cotoneaster—the West Bank by now supplies any desired amount of rooted cuttings. These were slow in establishing themselves, but did take hold over the course of three summers. At present both sides of the stairs are respectably cloaked in greenery, and I try to pretend that the asymmetry was a charming intention (to be perfectly honest, I try to distract attention from the whole arrangement). I am however hedging my bets by surrounding the (doomed?) junipers with inconspicuous but husky cotoneaster plantings as well; so far I'm keeping them cut back, but if the junipers do go eventually it will take only one or two seasons for the cotoneaster to cover the defect.

Two self-established clumps of wild blue flag soften the plainness of the cotoneaster planting on the one side; on the other, a clump of ferns, a good spread of Liatris (gayfeather), a few lemon lilies (this is an old-fashioned, spring-blooming daylily that I got from my mother's garden), a smattering of blue flag, and a small lilac bush constitute some seasonal variety and provide a transition to the blueberries that cover the rest of the hillside.

Weeds I Have Known

An area of some confusion in my developing relationship with my garden has been the question of what is a weed and what is a desirable plant; I haven't got it completely sorted out yet. I do abide by the classic definition that "a weed is any plant that is out of place," but I do not at all necessarily consider a plant out of place just because I didn't plant it there. Quite the contrary: In the kind of garden I have been aiming at, plants are very often placed by Mother Nature to far better aesthetic effect than I would have thought of, and in locations where even if I had thought of it I couldn't have made the plant grow (a blood-root blooming in the scanty debris accumulated in the fork of an old cedar tree, or a tiny pink leaning out of a stone wall with no visible root support at all). Some of the garden effects I am proudest of have designed and maintained themselves, and my pride relates only to the fact that I saw what was happening and let it go on.

Still, not *everything* goes, even in a wild garden, and my first maxim for a gardener would be "If you don't like weeding, don't garden." As the years have gone by and I introduce less and less new material into my grounds, a high proportion of the remaining maintenance consists of weeding. I have become, I consider, quite an expert on the weeds of this part of the world, and if it weren't for the pleasure of knowing myself to be (finally) so wise, I would blush at the realization that I brought in quite a few of them myself, in the enthusiasm of my wish to have a natural garden.

My two worst enemies made themselves known to me almost immediately, and by now I have an intimate knowledge of them and all their wicked little ways. One is called sheep sorrel, *Rumex acetosella*. It starts out as an agreeable little rosette of elongated leaves shaped like arrowheads, and in our first year on this property, when I knew nothing at all and had vast amounts of raw soil to cover, I actually planted a largish patch of this villain as a pleasant ground cover. (But it would have come anyway.) Once established, it sends out multiple infinitely-branched roots in all directions, and every root promptly produces a stem aboveground, and each stem grows to about ten inches high and flowers. The flowers, which are tiny but profuse, show as thin reddish plumes and seem perfectly innocuous, rather like the flowers on grasses. But they are followed by seeds. And if, in the already too busy month of June, you concentrate on pulling up all those flowering heads before they produce seeds, you don't have time to go systematically after the roots, which thus proceed merrily to extend their field of operations; and in another two months you are faced with a whole meadow of sorrel.

On the other hand, if you decide that this year for once you are going to get out every linear inch of root in one area before moving on, you get maybe a few square yards done, and all of a sudden it's October and there are *new* patches of sorrel, from seed, where there were none before—and now it's too cold to sit on the ground and work away at them.

Once this sheep sorrel gets into a planting that itself spreads by underground runners, it is hopeless in my experience to try to sort out the two kinds of roots. What works best for me in this situation is just to keep pulling off the new top growth of the sorrel every couple of weeks. As some wonderful book explained to me many years ago, no plant can live forever if you systematically deprive it of leaves, since photosynthesis for plants is like eating for animals, and takes place in green leaves. Usually, I find that three or four successive de-leafings will do the trick. But they have to be within a few weeks of each other; if you wait longer than that, the new leaves do produce enough energy to get the roots going again, and you're back where you started from.

The second most pernicious weed, in all parts of my garden, is the yellow wood sorrel, *Oxalis stricta*. In spite of the similarity in their common names—I think "sorrel" only refers to the fact that the leaves have a sour taste—this bears little superficial resemblance to the sheep sorrel. It is a seemingly delicate creature with dainty four-lobed leaves and rather pretty flowers of clear yellow. Like sheep sorrel, it spreads both by seeds and by underground roots, it is absolutely ubiquitous and just about ineradicable. In the Wild Garden I don't mind too much—up to a point. I just pull up the most massive growths in my twice-a-year rounds, and yank out particularly luxuriant single specimens where they are conspicuous and distracting. But in the Rock Garden I really have to take pains, and if I let a single season go by without settling down to this chore I am invariably sorry. This weed, all by itself, can make the whole miniature landscape look untidy, and any time spent in getting out every possible inch of tough white root is worth it.

Grass, in the wrong place, is a weed surprisingly difficult to deal with, having the characteristic of thriving on regular cutting-back, and not usually giving you its roots when you pull. The roots, also, go deeper than you would think for such fragile stems. The hand weeder is indispensable for grass, and where it has seeded into another ground cover to any significant degree, there is no alternative that I have been able to discover but to resign yourself to tracing back each individual grass stem and getting up its parent root. Once you have admitted this necessity, it is a not disagreeable activity (if you have the necessary time), and it does improve the look of things enormously.

Poison ivy infests this whole area but I don't find it a big problem to deal with, as it pulls up quite readily along with what seems to be *most* of its root. It doesn't take long to learn to recognize poison ivy in all stages of its life cycle; even the dead-looking winter stalks are unmistakable once you are well acquainted.

Other weeds that plague me here are wildflowers that I tried for a number of years to incorporate and include as regular members of the garden. But buttercups, daisies, goldenrod (except for the Seaside variety), Queen Anne's lace, Asiatic dayflower, hen-and-chickens, and cow vetch have all proven themselves too prolific, mainly by way of seeds, and also too much of a nuisance to eliminate (none of these plants except the Asiatic dayflower can be simply pulled up with the fingers). I feel like a traitor to the whole principle of natural gardening, but I try nowadays to keep these plants off my grounds except for the isolated suburb I call the Wildflower Border.

In the Wild Garden I introduced, early on, two perfectly charming wildflowers, one that came from the depths of the dark woods and the other a frequent colonizer of the roadsides around here. The first is called celandine—such a romantic, evocative name! Its fresh, elaborate greenery, up to eighteen inches high, and conspicuous yellow flowers do look romantic and are really attractive in shady places in the spring. But it turns out to be a Seeder, and much as I like it I don't want it *everywhere*, smothering everything else. While it pulls up fairly readily, it fills the bucket very fast (those pretty, deeply lobed leaves are surprisingly bulky) and a person can get tired of plodding up and down the hill to the compost pile after just so many trips. So I'm currently on an elimination campaign.

The same applies to jewelweed or touch-me-not, an incredibly rapid grower and spreader. Its single, nearly transparent stems, up to two feet high, and its pale green leaves make a rather orderly and innocent-looking show (only I do not appreciate such shows in the middle of my vinca or spoiling the lovely sweep of my ferns). Its half-inch orange blossoms, shining out of the dusk at twilight, do give the impression of so many jewels. But what makes this treasure a non-treasure is the characteristic for which it is named touch-me-not (*Impatiens capensis*): the ripe seedpods, along in late August, explode at a touch and spray seeds for at least five feet around. This is a delightful game if you are entertaining a three-year-old child, but you don't always have one of those at hand, and the jewelweed goes right on exploding and spraying whether anybody is there to watch or not and seems to have an extraordinarily high rate of germination. So it's off my list too, since there seems to be no way of having just a *little* of it. This is too bad.

A similar transformation has taken place in my feelings about wild strawberries, which I discovered with great joy in the Wild Garden's very first year and planted as a ground cover over a long stretch of bank. It made a fine ground cover, even retaining enough of its structure over the winter to prevent a bare look; and its pretty white flowers and bright red berries kept it interesting all summer, not to mention supplying the odd snack. But it *would not* keep to its allotted space; its rooted runners extended in all directions, and so fast it was just impossible to keep up with them; the path could not be kept clear; and, in general, there were enough other ground covers without the strawberries' invasiveness and somewhat messy uncontrolled appearance.

(Let me make it clear that I have no problem with ground covers in the paths per se, as long as they don't mind being walked on. The objection to things like strawberries is that their habit of growth results in multiple loops of tough stem above the ground, each loop being firmly fixed at both ends. For the unwary visitor, or the gardener loaded down with brush or buckets, the danger of tripping is serious and constant. Ground covers of this kind do have to be kept out of the walkways.)

In my early experimental days, when I was trying to find out what would grow best on an acid, dry, sandy soil, I was naturally delighted to learn about the sedum family. And indeed I have found good places for eight or ten different sedums, which please me by being of a good color or by having pretty flowers at the right time or by filling in bare places where nothing else will settle. But there is one—which like the others I got in a three-inch pot from the Farm and Garden nursery in New York, unlabelled, so I've never known its name—that I have regretted bitterly since its first summer. It's a sprawling, soft, spineless thing with "leaves" of a translucent yellow, which covers large areas very rapidly, with a sneaky air of crawling on its stomach when your back is turned. It has, briefly, an undistinguished yellow flower, but it never looks like anything, and it won't go away. It pulls up very readily, seeming hardly anchored to the earth, but of course, as with all sedums, any tiny piece that you leave behind proceeds to duplicate itself instantly. By now I have given up on it in areas of the Wild Garden that I don't get to often enough to give it the repeated systematic and total eradication that might free me of it; in smaller, more conspicuous places, with hard work, I have managed to do it in, or nearly so.

Another pest that I'm sorry to have introduced is the white wood aster. A stand of this, on a brilliantly sunny September day and from some distance, has a certain rough charm, especially since there is very little else in bloom at the time. But it spreads terribly, both underground (*very* hard to get up) and by seeds, and thus shows up all over your garden as irregularly distributed individual plants. And the blooms, which are scanty, are not really very attractive in close-up, being of a dirty white color and seeming always to be missing some of their teeth. In short, the thing looks like a weed and I am trying hard to eliminate it. I think I'll get there eventually, but it's slow going.

Bittersweet, around here, is a terrible weed, a fact it has taken me some time and much sad experience to learn. In the folly of my (gardening) youth I planted some bittersweet down by the roadside, in gravelly soil; I thought it would make a nice hedge and give me wonderful bouquets of orange-red berries in the fall. The plantings sulked for several years, and in the end I planted other things around them, assuming that they were defunct. But there came a rainy summer and the bittersweet revived and took over, sending out twining shoots up to twenty feet long that strangled anything they could get hold of. By the time I noticed what they were up to (I was concentrating on the upper garden that year) they had already killed the lower branches of a couple of big cedars and several major trunks in my favorite and biggest clump of bayberry. I rescued these poor things instantly, and pulled up the bittersweet for hours at a time (literally), but the next year there it was again, and so far I haven't ever managed to get back to it often enough in any one season to kill it. I have actually had nightmares about bittersweet.

(By the way, bittersweet berries are *not* good to bring into the house as bouquets; the berries fall uncontrollably and get squashed on the tablecloth or carpet, leaving ineradicable orange stains. Much better are barberry or cotoneaster, which have firm bright red berries well attached to their stems; or even the dusky umbels of the multiflora rose.)

We have other trailing and twining vines here. Hall's honeysuckle I have mentioned. I planted this along the driveway, years ago, following the recommendation of a book I'd liked. It moped and pined and made no progress at all and I forgot about it until the ivy ground cover to the south and the vinca ground cover to the north met over its prostrate form and provided, I suppose, some relief from the heat and dryness and maybe even some nutrition from their fallen leaves. Anyway, for some reason the honeysuckle suddenly took hold and the next thing I knew it was blooming cheerfully away up in the branches of the cedar and the shadbush and the highbush blueberry that border the drive just there, and making great snarls on the ground with the ivy and the vinca, to truly inartistic effect. So—as seems to happen to me disagreeably often—I had to spend several seasons wearily pulling out what I had worked so hard to establish.

Virginia creeper, which I brought in as a ground cover a long time ago, turns out not to be very good for that purpose. Although you see it on the ground in open country looking just fine, what it really wants to do is to climb up and through trees. In my garden it cannot be persuaded to cover ground if there is any chance of its going up anything vertical. It looks reasonably good on the trunks in the summer, and quite pretty in the autumn when the leaves turn bright red. But then they fall, and you're left with ropelike dangling stems that are most unattractive; and the new leaves don't come out until late in the spring. I now think Virginia creeper should be confined to large flat areas, or to draping itself casually over a stone wall or climbing up a simple post where it can be easily trimmed back. In a wooded area, in my opinion, it only causes frustration.

There is an annual creeper that seems to be getting more prevalent here (there have been two really wet summers). Its name, believe it or not, is "climbing false buckwheat" (*Polygonum scandens*) and it produces a delicate tracery of reddish stems and pale green leaves that get so long and so profuse that whole shrubs are hidden under them. I've had blueberry bushes that actually died, apparently by being deprived of sun, when I didn't rescue them in time. These sinister growths are pulled up very readily, which is gratifying except that it feels as if you're working with cobwebs. If you happen to get infested by this one, be sure to pull it up before the tiny greenish flowers have made their seeds, otherwise you will have all its children to deal with the next year. (This is a counsel of perfection; I know it can't be carried out in a normal gardening season.)

The weeds that I have described above are the principal troublemakers in my garden. There are, of course, scores of others—catbrier and chickweed and dandelion and toadflax spring to mind—but none quite so widespread and invasive and time consuming, and presenting such an overall threat to the plants one is trying to cherish.

There is, however, another whole category of native plants that I have reluctantly added to my own personal list of weeds— not that they present any particular problem in control, but just to distinguish them from desirable native plants, or what I think of as *real* wildflowers. These are all rather coarse in character for my small place, of indeterminate or positively ugly color, and of no special distinction for close viewing. They include milkweed, pokeweed, ironweed, joe-pyeweed, hardhack, Bouncing Bet, the native evening primrose, most of the local asters, and even the tall meadow rue. I have seen all these recommended for wild gardens. And I have, in my day, brought them all home and planted them and tried to think I liked the effect, but I don't. They may pass muster in an enormous meadow meant to be looked at from a distance, showing a more or less graceful sweep of misty color against the yellowish-green of the grasses, like the effect from a train window as you speed by; but they are not for intimate, everyday appreciation.

(Within this category, I do make an exception in the case of the tall yellow-flowered mullein. This, I admit, pops up in many spots where you don't want it and proceeds to smother everything in sight with its enormous felted white leaves, and this tendency has to be dealt with firmly. But it also has a talent for placing itself unexpectedly where its architectural presence lends drama to an otherwise dull spot, and for this virtue I allow it a limited freedom in my garden.)

Then there are the smaller things such as red and white clover, hen-and-chickens, ladies' tresses, and wild mustard. I've planted all of these too (yes, really, they have their points and it's always a question of what your alternatives are) but for me they don't pull their weight in garden value, and besides they are quite a nuisance to get rid of when you decide you don't want them anymore.

We have a wild plant all over this place, wherever it's shady, that rejoices in the name of "starry false Solomon's seal" (*Smilacina stellata*). It is hard to turn against a being whose name in two languages has such classical/romantic connotations that it practically constitutes the plot of an Italian opera, but I have finally done it. This plant is like a poor imitation of lily of the valley, only the leaves are smaller and shabbier and the blossoms aren't like little white bells and have no fragrance. Its offense is that it sets itself up as a ground cover but doesn't do the job adequately; its fat white roots make quite a close network underground, but only put up stems at intervals of ten to fifteen inches. So you can't leave it to be a ground cover all by itself, and if you try to be tactful and polite and let it combine with something like vinca or pachysandra, it interferes with their elegant tailored effect without adding any definitive attraction of its own.

The plant that is actually called "wild lily of the valley" doesn't look nearly as much like it as the smilacina; it's a low, neat, thickly growing thing with shiny two-inch leaves and a delicate white fluff of a blossom. This one makes definitive large mats and *does* know how to be a ground cover. Its name is *Maianthemum canadense*. I don't count this one among the weeds; in fact, I have encouraged it wherever it has shown up. It doesn't transplant well.

I have one final piece of advice on the subject of weeding; it's important, and it was years before I learned it. Do your weeding only after a substantial rain, or water the area very thoroughly the day before you plan to tackle it. It will cut your weeding time in half, and greatly increase the proportion of roots that will yield to fingers alone. When you come to think of it, you will realize the difference there naturally *would* be between pulling things out of mud and pulling them out of soil that is baked hard. But maybe you haven't come to think of it yet, as I didn't. So I am pointing it out.

The Blueberry Bushes

I have mentioned that the native plants already on our property when we arrived included three kinds of blueberries,
which I have called high, regular, and low. The regular bushes
are the only ones that produce edible berries; they are good, but
we rarely have a chance to taste them since the birds eat them all
up well before they are ripe from a human point of view. As the
idea of protecting the berries with netting strikes me as a de-
secration of the landscape unless one is growing blueberries for
a living, I resigned myself from early on to the fact that these
were not *our* berries; they were to be thought of only as lures for
bird life.

We have only one of the high bushes left, along the driveway near the house. The low bushes (about a foot high) are all in one area near the western border of the property, and serve to face down the rhododendrons that define the property line and keep us and our neighbors from looking into each other's windows. But the regular bushes stretch across nearly the whole width of the property in its northern third, in an irregular band that is from twenty to fifty feet across. It is almost a "pure culture," having—originally—only a few wild chokeberries and an occasional stunted bayberry to vary its expanse.

We had to make two paths through this little plantation the first thing, simply to provide access to the northern end of the property on both sides. Otherwise we left it pretty much as it was for a number of years; then interesting things began to happen.

The first thing was that when we added on to the existing house, one of the additions was a new living room with big windows facing north. For the first time I found myself looking directly at the blueberries, and for the first time realized that the planting ws not good to look at on a close-up and prolonged basis. The chokeberries, slim uninspiring trees—I suppose you'd call them trees since they had single stems, even though they were only seven or eight feet high—had pretty blossoms in the spring, but only for about a week; the rest of the time they just sat there spoiling the uniform height of the blueberry plantation. So I cut them all down. Then, I became aware—and I really don't know whether it was just a question of my becoming aware, or whether it was a new condition—that there was a significant amount of other material growing in amongst the blueberries. Upon investigation, there turned out to be, besides the few bayberries: young wild cherry trees; poison ivy; bittersweet; sumac; Carolina roses; bush honeysuckle; brambles; and a surprising amount of goldenrod of several varieties.

At that period I was enjoying the assistance of two high school youths, who gave me the benefit of their considerable muscle two days a week during the summer. (Those were wonderful days.) It was the work of about three weeks for the two of them to clear out all this miscellany, yanking it up by the roots wherever they could, and leaving a beautiful clean spread of just blueberries. Big sigh of relief and pleasure.

By late in the next spring, it became apparent that it wasn't that simple; all the interlopers were back, none the worse for their little setback. Some, indeed, seemed to think they had been pruned for their health and were putting out four stems for every one that had been cut off. The boys were busy making stone steps down below and clearing out brush from some other places, and I didn't send them back there until the fall, when they went through the whole process again. And to make a long and painful story short, cleaning out the blueberries once a year has proven to be of no value at all. For the past three years I've done it twice a year (I myself; the boys have faded into history) with no perceptible effect; and for next year I have determined I'll go all out, give this project the top priority, and go in there for twenty minutes or so every single day (of the four days a week that I'm here), moving round and round among the blueberries so as to get each new shoot in its infancy and not give it any chance at all to gather its strength together to make new root growth.

This is a fairly dismal prospect. Cleaning out these bushes is not one of my preferred gardening jobs, combining as it does strenuous arm work with standing at most inconvenient angles and frequent stooping and searching, all in amongst the spiny tangled undergrowth that pulls your glasses off and scratches your face, in order to get your clippers right down to the base of the stem you're after and leave no remnant aboveground to start new growth. But unpleasant as it is, it seems to be unavoidable.

The blueberries, when they *are* kept clean, are surprisingly decorative in themselves, in addition to their function as an enclosure for the Rock Garden. Their wood has a distinct reddish tinge, which in winter gives a warm heathery look to the whole mass, in agreeable contrast to the dark smoky-green cedar spires and the buff-colored expanses of mown grass. Against this background the nearly black trunks and branches of three wild cherry trees in different parts of the prospect appear as distinct meaningful figures. In spring the new blueberry growth is vividly red, much more striking than the blossoms that come later. And the leaves, too, before falling in November, show flaming red for several weeks. So you get quite a lot of what the books call "color and incident," but all at a relatively subtle harmonious level, in keeping with the tone of this peaceful landscape.

Furthermore the blueberries shelter a remarkable variety of animal and bird life. Both quail and goldfinches have nested there; a great many other birds come for the berries or to peck seeds from the ground. Small animals in variety forage on its edges, and we have seen foxes three times, slinking through the undergrowth. I enjoy having this miniature piece of ecology right under my eyes, and would hate to lose it. It is worth a good deal of trouble.

A Few Plagues and Pests

Like many another liberally educated idealist, I began my dealings with the land in the innocent conviction that it would be cooperation all the way. I would do my bit and make things easy for Nature, and Nature would, in respectful gratitude, confine herself to producing only salutary and delightful life forms within my domain. I was totally against using poisons on my property. And, in principle, I still am; I do so only under the severest provocation.

But I have my limits. To confess them and get them out of the way immediately, there are two kinds of animal against whom I have found chemical action necessary. One is the slug, whose malevolent cohorts regularly eat up my maidenhair ferns and who get into almost everything in the Wild Garden and even, in a wet season, in a place as normally arid as the Rock Garden. Their depredations are not only unsightly but killing. Moreover, the sensation of putting your hand to the ground for support while you're weeding and encountering something wet and cold but obviously alive is . . . disconcerting; when it happens over and over in a given morning it gives rise to a feeling of persecution and horror. I've tried the ploy of putting out beer in a saucer for them to get drunk and drown in, but they never came and got it. (It is true, though, that the beer cans I pick up on the roadside and rinse for recycling frequently have several slugs inside, so there must be something to this approach.) What does seem to work is a commercial snail-and-slug killer in pellet form; this is apparently highly toxic to birds and animals as well as humans, so I sprinkle it only sparingly, under a covering of live leaves, and only when the slug population is so dense that I'm frantic. I am glad to say that this has been necessary only about four times in the past twenty years.

The other creature that, on rare occasions, has to be poisoned is the Japanese beetle. Why it doesn't make a nuisance of itself *every* year I don't know, but the fact is that it, too, usually stays within the limits of tolerability. I call it *in*tolerable when the leaves on my rosebushes and wisteria vine have been three-quarters eaten away and the plant seems in imminent danger of dying; at that point I decide that Nature's defenses are not enough, and use an all-purpose rose spray. Although the directions (and the books written by professional rosarians) say to repeat this every few weeks, I have never done it more than once in a season. The beetles disappear and don't return; why should I do anything more?

Earthworms, of course, I have in plenty, and I know people who consider *them* pests. They, too, can give you a start when you lay your hand on them unexpectedly. But as any gardener knows, they, unlike slugs, are actually good for plants as they keep the soil well aerated, and fertilize it with their excretions. You come, eventually, to perceive them as beneficent little pet-like creatures and completely lose your "instinctive" sense of repulsion, just as you come eventually to think of compost in altogether positive terms as a delectable, wholesome substance rather like chocolate cake, oblivious to its known origins in death, dirt, and decay.

Tent caterpillars turn up every now and then, but so far haven't required any drastic property-wide action. When individual tents appear I just cut off the involved branch and burn it. They haven't been a real problem, nor have the multitudinous ants, wasps, and bees—at least, not as far as the garden is concerned. I have twice found bees' nests in the compost pile, and once in the West Bank, and I have learned that human beings, even females of a certain age, can run faster than bees can fly, a comforting thing to know. (What my husband does with bees' nests is to pour paint-thinner into them. This doesn't seem to affect the nutritional quality of the compost, though it reduces the pleasure of working with it for a few weeks.)

There are leaf miners that make fascinating whitish tracks all over the columbine leaves, more some years than others. They don't destroy enough of the leaf substance to present any threat to the life of the plant, and I don't do anything about them.

The only other small organisms that have bothered my plantings are viruses. As I have already recounted, blights have killed extensive establishments of forget-me-nots and large banks of prostrate juniper, as well as most of my beloved dogwood trees. The only reasonable reaction to such tragedies is a philosophical one, sweetened with the compensatory thought that there is now an opportunity for planting something new.

There are (at least) two microorganisms that inhabit my place as harmless parasites, living on other plants without killing or even seriously harming them. One of these is the "rust" fungus that affects our cedar trees. It produces soft doughy masses of a brilliant orange color that drip in gobbets from the trunk and branches and lie around on the ground like materializations from another planet. This fungus is seeking, they say, for a host for the next part of its life cycle, which involves the apple tree; in the apple tree it does do damage and spoils the crop. So you can never plant apple and cedar trees in the same neighborhood, and that is one reason I haven't planted any flowering crabapples or even any ordinary eating apples. (The other is that the native wild cherries serve, to my mind, very much the same decorative purposes that apple trees would do, and don't have to be sprayed. They do, however, suffer from a fungus of their own that causes unsightly, slowly-enlarging black oozing sores on the trunks and branches. The local nurseryman says there is no cure for this, and I just prune off the affected branches.)

The other parasite is unknown to me by name. It affects the mountain laurels that grow on the shady east side of the house, causing brown spots on their leaves. This doesn't seem to do any significant damage; the leaves don't even drop off. It is unattractive but I haven't come across any advice on what to do about it so I try to ignore it.

Of larger life forms we have garter snakes, toads, field mice, chipmunks, red and gray squirrels, rabbits, skunks, moles, woodchucks, raccoons, opossums, and—rarely—foxes. Also, numerous dogs and cats belonging to our neighbors. These animals cause surprisingly little trouble, although I suspect that my difficulties in growing crocuses are related to the well-known penchant of squirrels and chipmunks for their bulbs, and I have more than once seen a young rabbit chewing up a crocus in full bloom—leaves, blossoms, and all. The skunks (or the woodchucks?) like to make snout tracks in the lawn, but these heal readily. And on the whole I like the feeling that we are sharing the place with its original denizens and haven't evicted them altogether; I enjoy the sense, and the occasional glimpse, of their presence. I think, however, that if I were ever again to try to grow vegetables, something in the way of a high barbed-wire enclosure would be in order, preferably with two armed guards on twenty-four hour duty.

I suppose the reason for my nearly complete freedom from disease and pest problems probably has to do with my relaxed, not to say shiftless, ways. I am, after all, growing mostly native material, long acclimatized to this environment. And I don't force it in any way; if it's willing to grow on this property I let it, pretty much, grow where and as it likes. I keep it reasonably free from overcrowding, but I don't stimulate it into overly lush growth with chemical fertilizers, or encourage it to exhaust itself in bloom. And it is my contention that this adequate-but-not-luxurious approach to the care and feeding of my garden results in relatively slow-growing, hardy, long-lived plants that are comparatively disease-resistant. Whether this contention is founded in scientific fact, I don't know, but underfeeding humans is said to be the single best way to ensure a long healthy life, and it *may* be true of plants as well. As far as insects are concerned, it seems likely that the large number of birds we attract do their share in keeping the bug population down.

It is also true that I don't *look* for diseases. If the plant can stand up, and bloom, and hold its own against its neighbors, and come back the next year, I don't really care if it has a few pimples or a gall or two; I am not trying to produce superplants or to win prizes.

In short, my attitude is a rather simpleminded and primitive one. In keeping with this, I live in superstitious dread of the fire blight which is said to come like a thief in the night and lay waste your cotoneasters in no time at all, nor can any remedy prevail against it. What I would do with those large expanses of sunny bank if *both* my spreading junipers *and* the cotoneasters decided to die I cannot bear to contemplate. I just pray to the gods of gardening that it will not be so.

Birds in My Garden

Birds, like gardening, had never been part of my conscious life until we came to Rhode Island; there were simply no hooks in my mind on which to hang information about birds, so that any knowledge I had accidentally been exposed to up to that point had failed to register. But at Woodwinds there was bird-input of a new order of magnitude that even I could not ignore.

What drew—demanded—my attention first of all was the astonishing racket they made just before dawn every morning. We had been accustomed, for some years, to sleeping through the traffic noises of a major avenue in mid-Manhattan, in close proximity to three hospitals; but in the country we were regularly awakened by the birds for many months, until we finally adjusted to that, too. Similarly, in all my time outdoors at Woodwinds, especially in the spring, I was overwhelmed by the nearly continuous barrage of birdcalls and birdsongs, their variety and their sheer volume. It was impossible not to get a little curious about this or that repeated hierophantic cry, and finally I began acquiring bird books and ransacking the Westerly Library to find out what it was all about. This was one more dimension in the mysterious inner life of the garden, and I developed quite a fever for it over several years.

One immediate result of my reading was the realization that the more clearing of trees and underbrush there was going to be, on our own as well as neighboring properties, the less space there would be to accommodate bird life. I found that each kind of bird tends to have a specific minimum area that can normally sustain one pair with its young; for most species, our own little property couldn't hope to be the home for more than one pair at best, and I wanted to retain this precious potential as far as I could. I had no control over what our neighbors did, but I determined to maintain our own bit of land, to some degree, as a hospitable habitat for the birds.

Accordingly, in the course of laying out the proposed "development" of various areas, I designated the entire northeast corner of the property, an area about thirty by seventy feet, as the Bird Sanctuary. We have left this essentially untouched, a jungle of all the native growths in free competition. Other parts of the grounds may still be called "wild" but they are, in fact, extensively pruned and groomed and no longer offer much in the way of tangled undergrowth in which birds can range undisturbed and raise their little ones free from predators. A "wild garden," at least as I have interpreted it, is not so very wild after all.

120

I will admit that my motives for choosing this particular section as a bird habitat were mixed. Lying as it does at the very highest point of our land, and sloping steeply downward to the east, it presents even more formidable barriers to horticulture than other parts of our property. The rocks are even larger and more irregular, the soil between them even thinner. Somehow this feeble substrate manages to support a considerable thicket of ten-foot shrubbery as well as a large number of healthy cedar trees, and intertwining vines—of five different kinds—enough for Tarzan of the Apes. But to reduce this thicket to manageability and replace it with an east-facing Alpine rock garden (an idea that I toyed with for some months) would have been a labor dwarfing all my other efforts; I simply didn't think it was doable, by me, in this lifetime. And still another factor was the ideal placement of this large and still growing thicket in relation to the house, making it a perfect windbreak for the winter storms that come almost without exception from the northeast. Indeed, I think my Rock Garden, and the few roses I have planted on the east slope near the parking area, have been saved more than once by the intervention of that friendly barrier of cedars and shrubbery.

The brush borders that mark our property lines to east and west, and the large expanse of blueberry bushes, present modified versions of this bird habitat; I try to keep them sufficiently groomed for decency, but still leave as much thickness and entanglement as possible within the limits of what is really offensive to look at, for the shelter and encouragement of the birds.

The natural growth of our hillside is almost ideal for birds from the point of view of their food supply. The berries of cedars, honeysuckles, blueberries and bayberries, rugosa roses, and even poison ivy are all tremendous favorites and hang on through the winter, being especially crucial for the many species that refuse to come near the house for the food I put out. And when planting new things, I give preference always—other things being equal—to plants whose seeds will attract the birds. I do *not* leave flower stems standing all winter, even though the seeds would be good for the birds; they are just too bedraggled looking. But there are plenty of goldenrods and asters and other wildflowers in the Bird Sanctuary corner; there are seeds from shrubs and vines; and I do put out massive amounts of compensatory seeds on the deck.

I feed the birds both summer and winter. In neither season does this arise from conservationist zeal; I simply want to persuade the birds to come closer and alight for a few minutes at a time so I (and my friends and relations) can appreciate their beauty and their individual style, as well as their songs. In summer I hang two large cylindrical feeders from the branches of the wild cherry tree that arches over the Rock Garden. One holds mixed seeds and the other sunflower seeds. As many of our birds prefer the sunflower seeds, the mixed ones tend to be flung aside impatiently and, in spite of the saucer conveniently arranged at the base of the cylinder to catch them, a large number end up on the ground among the blueberry bushes, where they are much relished by those species that would rather eat from the ground anyway. The combined appeal of these two feeders and the birdbath only a dozen feet away keeps the Rock Garden a lively place all summer long, providing exactly the right level of entertainment to humans sitting on the terrace with gin and tonics or cups of tea, or sometimes with nothing at all in hand, only beach-glazed eyes and peacefully vacant minds.

In winter these feeders are taken down and the birdbath—whose concrete might otherwise crack in a freeze—is brought into the garage, its space being retained and its function to some degree continued by a large aluminum pan. The big living room, whose windows look out onto the terrace and the Rock Garden, is seldom occupied during the day in the winter; the focus of domestic life, until sundown, is the south-facing family room, surrounded on three sides by a wide deck. From the roof of this deck I have hung a great variety of bird feeders, almost all of which have been promptly destroyed by weather or by pecking or by mauling on the part of squirrels or (at night) raccoons. Only two kinds have survived the treatment they get from my muscular furred and feathered friends: one is the plastic cylinder with metal reinforcements at top and bottom and around the feeding holes, and the other is a plain but sturdy open rectangle made of wood, measuring about two by two-and-a-half feet, with a removable insert consisting of a framed piece of wire screening. All of these hold seeds; some birds (such as cardinals and mourning doves) have a strong preference for the flat, open feeder, whereas others (like chickadees and finches) flock to the vertical ones.

Some birds, especially those whose normal diet includes insects, are very fond of fatty foods, and some are said to enjoy fresh or dried fruit. On my deck, both suet and peanut butter are consumed rapidly. There are a number of ingenious contraptions for offering these delicacies to the birds while still frustrating the squirrels; at Woodwinds, the squirrels have invariably won out in the end. They tear the small wire or plastic-mesh feeders apart or pull them away from their attachments, and gnaw the intricate wooden ones to splinters. Even a squirrel guard doesn't help on the deck, as they leap from the railing and land *underneath* the guard.

So I have resigned myself to feeding squirrels as well as birds, though they eat a great deal more. (I refuse to feed raccoons; but they are easily foiled by bringing the fatty feeders in at night.) The best feeder I ever had for this kind of offering was one my father made: a cylindrical section of a rough-barked tree branch, about five inches in diameter, with several shallow holes drilled in it, three inches wide by one inch deep, which could be filled with peanut butter or rendered suet. This was hung by a heavy wire fastened to long strong screws near the top of the log, and lasted for four or five years; eventually the bark was pulled off, the holes gnawed out of all recognition and usefulness, and the screws dislodged. I have subsequently made shift with sections of ordinary firewood, smearing the peanut butter or suet straight on to the bark, and hanging the section with screws and a wire as before. It's a functional arrangement, having the advantage that when the squirrels have taken all they can there is still some fat left in the bark crevices for the birds. But it doesn't hold up for long.

Besides ordinary suet, I find both birds and squirrels are extremely partial to the hardened grease that congeals on the top of a pot of homemade soup; and it's nice not to have to throw this out. Sometimes I soften it and smear it on a bark log as I've described; sometimes I just put the hardened pieces on the railing, where the squirrels come immediately and eat them like cookies, holding them in both paws and nibbling round and round the edges.

For several years I had four feeders, containing various kinds of delicacies, suspended over the deck. They were immensely popular and supported a constantly amusing show; but since birds habitually combine their intake functions with those of excretion in a highly uncivilized way, the deck planking became grossly unappealing. As I had no interest in providing stable-boy services in return for entertainment, I was obliged to change the location of the hanging feeders; they are now suspended from several metal poles, ingeniously attached to the

deck-railing supports so as to lean outward at a forty-five degree angle. Thus the birds, while feeding, are not over the deck
at all, but rather fifteen feet above the lawn. I mention this
problem and its successful solution in case any of my readers are
contemplating the establishment of bird-feeding stations over
an area where humans will need to walk. This is not advisable.

In bird books you will read about special kinds of feeders,
and special foods, for certain much desired birds. I had seen
goldfinches around and was taken with the idea of giving them
their supposedly favorite food of thistle seeds, in a feeder specially designed to dispense these particularly small seeds. I still
have goldfinches, but none has ever (to my knowledge) come to
the thistle-seed feeder, either in its summer location right over
the blueberry bushes or its winter location on the deck. We do
have quite a number of wild thistles growing on the property; I
rather like them and have let them stay when they turn up in
unobtrusive corners where I won't have to weed around their
spiny leaves and stems: It may be that the goldfinches prefer
their thistle seeds fresh from the vine, as it were. In any case I
have stopped serving the expensive thistle seed; it was, for my
particular population, not appreciated.

The same lack of success has attended my efforts to bring
hummingbirds within good viewing distance. They are around;
I see them nearly every summer, and once found a nest down by
the roadside. I had seen them sipping from the blossoms of my
red coralbells when they were some distance from the house;
but when I moved the coralbells to the Rock Garden the hummingbirds failed to follow. I have actually seen them in the Rock
Garden, tasting everything *but* the coralbells.

I then resorted to modern technology and hung a scientifically designed hummingbird feeder from the wild cherry
tree behind the Rock Garden; I've also tried it, for months at a

time, hanging on the deck. Goldfinches have visited it rather commonly (!), but never a hummingbird. I thought these locations were perhaps too high for the hummingbirds to perceive them as flowers, and hung one from a two-foot metal rod stuck into the ground in a corner of the Rock Garden. Two seasons passed without a single visit from a hummingbird. As it is rather a nuisance to keep this feeder filled and cleaned, I have now retired it.

The birds that lived here before we came presumably were always able to find places to nest, and I haven't been concerned for them beyond leaving that northeast corner for their use. But I read a good deal about the plight of bluebirds, who like holes in the trunks of old trees or wooden fence posts, and are dying out because of the paucity of these items in today's too-well-groomed, metal-fenced landscapes. Not having seen a bluebird since my extreme youth, and remembering them as extraordinarily appealing little creatures, I have put up two bluebird houses near the property line to north and west, in locations corresponding as closely as I can manage to the bluebirds' supposedly preferred locations, very early in the spring as recommended. Every year for the last six or seven years, both houses are occupied within half a day—by house wrens. These are perfectly agreeable tenants and well worth their rent in entertainment value, with their frenetic nest-building followed by raising up to three families in one season, all accompanied by truly beautiful bursts of song. But I'd like, just once, to get a bluebird family.

One year a tree swallow began to settle in (there are hundreds of them in the neighborhood, skimming low over the golf course at dusk to feast on mosquitoes). He invited his mate and they began to build, only to be set upon by a house wren in the full fury of his own nesting fever. It was a short and unequal contest, from which the swallows retired with dignity, leaving the wren to strut insufferably in front of his wife. Such episodes, into which it is easy to read quasi-human characteristics, are among the enjoyments of keeping half an eye on the birds.

I also provide, specifically for the wrens, a tiny house with a red roof that hangs from a branch just over the corner of the parking area, looking entirely comfortable and homey between the lilac bush and the roses and making a pretty picture for everyone who drives up. This too is promptly occupied each year, but as it is at some distance from the house I don't follow its domestic fortunes closely.

All the birdhouses—which are sturdily made of plain unfinished cedar, with the single exception of the smallest, whose roof is stained red—are taken down in the fall, emptied, and stored in the garage over the winter. It is usual to find at least two twiggy nests in them, one on top of the other; and not uncommon at all to see, at the very top, a softer nest lined with moss and down and hair, in which are peacefully resting a family of infant field mice, curled up and pink. I turn them out into the garden and hope I have not consigned them to immediate death. It is hard not to feel like a villain doing this, when their parents have taken such pains to provide a snug warm home for the winter. But although I'm quite tolerant of mice around the place (as long as they stay out of the house), I draw the line at subsidizing their housing and thus artificially encouraging their proliferation.

When I learned from my bird-reading that a single purple martin could eat tens of thousands of mosquitoes in a day, I hastened to erect a two-story, twelve-family house on a twenty-foot pole, away up on the edge of the golf course. For four years it went up early in the spring (so as to catch the attention of the "scouts" the martins are said to send out looking for likely nesting sites), and came down in the fall, but no purple martins ever came near us. I had all the work and none of the benefit, since the apartments were occupied to their limit by families of house finches and required quite arduous cleaning at the end of each summer. Finally it began to seem hopeless, and I was tired of explaining to my golfing friends that there were really no purple martins in my purple-martin house, which made me feel like a humbug. So it came down.

Our house construction includes a large number of wide horizontal beams under the deck, divided into cubbies by vertical partitions. These are irresistible to robins, and one or two families each season are the rule. It is something of a nuisance having them quite so much with us; every time I come around a corner the mother robin squawks and takes herself off with a wild flurry of wings, giving me a great startle, which I have never learned to control. But it is fun to watch the babies being fed, and growing up, and plopping around on the lawn in the sophomoric complacency of having just learned to fly but infinitely preferring not to.

In the depression to the east of us red-winged blackbirds nest nearly every year; I have seen two orioles' nests swaying in the poplar trees across the road; and one memorable summer an enterprising crow built a home in the top of our tallest cedar tree. For a couple of weeks I thought, from the hideous cries filling the air to the south of the house, that a large predator was attacking a whole colony of wild geese, or that some other calamity of similar proportions was overtaking a major bird community. But one day I tracked the noise to its source and found the crow's nest, and realized that whereas the nestlings of other species make their wants known by saying "peep-peep," or at most "CHEEP-CHEEP," the baby crow *roars* like a spawn of

128

Hell. I have heard these cries in subsequent years, but, thank goodness, never again on our own grounds.

Mockingbirds are our most accomplished singers. I was surprised to find them so far north, but they have apparently taken over this entire part of the country. In spring, especially when there is a full moon, they really do sing nearly all night, most musically and movingly and with never a repeated phrase. Their cousins the catbirds can match them in single phrases (each repeated once) for a brief sequence, but never pour out those very long liquid soliloquies, and don't sing at night. Robins, wrens, song sparrows, and even house finches in the spring are all good singers; and I personally enjoy the constant background murmur, monotonous but graceful, of the mourning dove, and even the martial "here I am" signal of the bobwhite.

Altogether, I have checked off more than forty species in my *Audubon Land Bird Guide* as having been seen at least once. About thirty-five of these are regular inhabitants, and a few are very rare visitors. Among the latter is the small snowy owl who sat in a tree and watched my husband pacing out the dimensions of the house site, one winter's day in 1969. We have seen no owls since then and I would be inclined to doubt my husband's story except that he was clever enough to photograph the bird. It would seem that we did oust at least one of the native population; I'm not aware of any others.

I have not even mentioned, because strictly speaking they are not a part of "my garden," the dozens of water birds that thrive in this area; they include the enormous colonies of swans that are a major tourist attraction, the kingfishers and herons one occasionally sees on the edges of the salt marshes, the large flocks of wild geese of all kinds, and the now numerous families of ospreys nesting on specially erected platforms set up on high poles near the shore. All these, though living relatively far from our immediate property, are regularly seen (and often heard) overhead and supply us with an extra measure of ornamentation. They are, as far as I am concerned, a free gift, a special kind of "borrowed view," for which I am duly grateful.

In our generally quiet and subdued landscape, the birds give a needed touch of vivacity, and even of company. Now that I've become more aware of them as a group and learned to recognize the characteristics of individual species, I tend in most of my outdoor activities to keep one set of (largely unconscious) antennae on the alert, monitoring what is going on in the bird world. In sitting back to appreciate a particular landscape picture I notice, besides the plant material, the movement and color of the birds inhabiting it; I hear, on the edge of my mind, the bluejays calling back and forth to each other; I am aware of scuffling in the shrubbery, or the quiet rustle of dry leaves as a quail scratches his way along. Without particularly trying to, I have learned to know a chickadee by its flight and a mockingbird by its preening gait. I recognize the "chip! chip!" of an excited cardinal and the plaintive mewing of the catbird.

All these intimations of parallel existences I find enormously enriching, often diverting, sometimes dramatic (as when a cloud of migrating starlings several thousand strong darkens the sky and then takes over the property for two or three hours, during which I am literally afraid to go outside, and after which the cedars are visibly denuded of their beautiful blue berries). Birds, even more than rabbits and squirrels, somehow populate the garden and give it meaning that is related to the deep patterns of life.

The Wildflower Border

Our land is bordered on the east by a vacant lot full of cedar trees and brush. The driveway wanders up the eastern slope, about fifteen feet from the property line at its beginning, and a mere four feet by the time it reaches the level where the house is built. Brush and ground cover come right to the driveway in its lower part, but after sixty feet or so this growth recedes, leaving a swath of mown grass where we once kept a boat and that we still call the Boat Cubby. This swath terminates, on the east, in a mixed growth of cedars, bayberries, honeysuckle, and low blueberries that marks the property line itself, and from our first arrival I have tried to invent some way of "furnishing" this border so as to indicate that it was still part of civilization, and to begin to denote the approach to the house.

In the beginning I made a scanty planting of vinca in the thin stony ground along the whole stretch, and for several years weeded it and even fertilized it, but it didn't seem interested so I lost interest, too. I had a bunch of beautiful blue irises from my mother's garden that didn't seem to fit anywhere else, and I deposited them "temporarily" at the foot of the telephone pole that unfortunately sits right beside the road there. Then my attention was diverted, for several years, to other areas.

But there came a day when I dug up an enormous clump of Siberian iris that was in the wrong spot and there turned out to be no right spot for it, so I simply dumped it under the stand of bayberries in the middle of this "border," as a temporizing measure one step short of actually throwing it on the compost. I literally dumped it, with no ground preparation and no fertilizer and no water, only its own root ball—and the next spring it came up as heartily as ever and bloomed cheerfully, and continued to do so for several more years, until it was killed off by a long drought. I wasn't sorry to see it go, having lost my interest in these irises (I much prefer the wild blue flag, and it sits better in my landscape); but its determined though temporary survival under no care whatsoever brought back some ideas I thought I had abandoned.

Presently I had to reduce the size of an overenthusiastic group of native daylilies, and couldn't bear to throw *them* away, and I scratched some inadequate saucers in the ground in the same area, just enough to hold them in position, and left them alone, and they thrived and spread. And I had some American columbine that didn't bloom well in the shade of the Wild Garden, and I moved a few plants to the same area with the same lack of "good practice," and *they* thrived and spread. And more and more I found I had plants that there was no place for but that I couldn't quite bring myself to destroy: wildflowers like the Queen Anne's lace and buttercups and coreopsis and Deptford pinks that were too invasive for the more controlled part of my garden, but that I wanted to have around somewhere. I stuck them, or seeded them, into this border.

I divided some clumps of Christmas fern and found myself with twenty young plants, and stuck them in; I sent away for fifty lily bulbs "for naturalizing" and stuck them in. I stuck in bits of sedum and pinks and thyme gleaned from cleaning up other areas, and leftover evening primroses and violets that had sprung up where they weren't wanted. Foxgloves and mulleins moved in by themselves. I added two large clumps of wild asters that bloom in October, producing a cloud of small white stars, too ragged and bulky for any other location but quite effective here where you see them at some distance while driving past. With all these colonists spreading and seeding at their own pleasure (none of them seems to care at all about the inadequate soil), over about three years there came into blurry focus a sort of fantastic irregular border, which is now about sixty feet in length though only two feet deep so far.

I call this my Wildflower Border, but that's a slight misnomer. Besides the lily bulbs (which are already deteriorating), I have put in a number of plants from the catalogs that I can't resist but have no real place for, colorful things with small bright blooms over a long period, pink and red Achilleas and Moonbeam coreopsis and low-growing scarlet geraniums. All of these are planted with minimal ceremony, or just seeded into lightly scratched soil, and are given only grudging amounts of water in direst need; when there is any compost left over I add a skimpy layer but I don't worry if there isn't any.

I do pull up grass a couple of times a year, but otherwise my principle has been to start a whole lot of tough self-sufficient things and let them fight it out. Anything that can't handle the conditions, or the competition, doesn't belong here. This principle has been effective in this location (though it wasn't in the Gravel Pit), and has resulted in a rather appealing patchwork of mixed color through most of the spring, summer, and fall. In winter there is enough Christmas fern and vinca to define the area (I cut down all the dead wildflower stems as soon as they have cast their seeds), and altogether this is one of the more satisfactory of my projects.

The border is well placed in relation to the propensity of its inhabitants to spread hither and yon. They don't come up in the underbrush behind them because it's too shady; if they come up in the grass toward the driveway they get mown down; and they are at least seventy feet from any other planted area where their seeds might be a nuisance. So it isn't a problem to keep them within bounds.

Contrary to the dire predictions of those who tell you you must *never* plant without a plan, the Wildflower Border—which I like to think resembles the flowering unmown roadsides of my rural youth—is perfectly pleasing. It looks quite unforced, as if the flowers just happened to spring up at the sunny edge of the thicket, but nonetheless has a certain casual charm. I have even added a couple of chairs and a small table under the cedars surrounding the Boat Cubby, where the driveway swings away from the property line, so as to admire the effect on hot afternoons.

The Seasons

In the beginning I thought of gardening as a strictly summer-time occupation, something I would only concern myself with during the growing season, when things had to be fed and pinched back and weeded and generally mothered along. Once the last flowers of October faded I reluctantly put the garden out of my mind as something I could productively interact with, and resigned myself to five months or so of frustration. One of my favorite old gardening books has a chapter entitled "Winter, Damn It," and that's about the way I felt.

But that attitude, like so many of those I started out with, has changed drastically. Year after year, I found there wasn't time enough to do everything in the few warm months; year after year, I'd come out of my cocoon at the end of March and find things that should have been taken care of while the plants were dormant. I began to grasp the reality of what the books were saying about winter activities, and finally it penetrated to me that gardening is a year-round enterprise, at least if you want to produce anything more interesting than big solid blocks of flowers.

My gardening year begins immediately after Christmas, when the new seed and nursery catalogs arrive. Although I still read these through with great care and turn down many corners and make many notes, I am fairly abstemious these days when it comes to actually ordering things. In the early years I found the offerings almost irresistible and ordered with great abandon as to variety but only one, two, or three of each kind of plant due to the fact that nearly everything was for me an unknown and an experiment. Thus I often wound up with tiny spots of unrelated this and that, here and there, with nothing making any significant impression. Nowadays, being both wiser and shorter of time for things to multiply, I tend to order each spring a goodly number of some one kind of plant I've decided I want for a particular place, so that a respectable little plantation is established at once. (For larger things, and when I'm not fussy about the exact variety, I use the local nurseries to get larger specimens and avoid the vicissitudes of transportation.)

The other winter activity is pruning. In this area there are plenty of days even in midwinter when the temperature is in the forties and fifties, the most comfortable weather for heavy work. With leaves gone, it is easy to see the structural conformation of trees and shrubs, and to identify those outlying or unshapely branches that should be taken off. According to the books, the plant doesn't lose sap when you trim it during the winter, whereas in warmer weather it may "bleed" quite pro-

fusely, to the detriment of its health. And finally, the ground in winter is free of soft foliage like that of ferns and bulbs, so that walking around and under the things you are trying to prune is easier and doesn't harm the looks of the garden.

So on every reasonably clement day through January, February, and March I bundle up in as many layers as seems judicious and go out to groom my surroundings. This has a number of advantages besides just getting the pruning done. Somehow, without the distraction of green and blossoming things, I see the garden in a different way. I become aware of its skeleton, its "design," the relationship of one part to another, the proportions of parts to the whole. And then, once I'm out there I tend to start doing other little chores, like picking up blown-down branches and moving stones into better positions. And I meditate on possibilities for new plantings or rearrangements of old ones, and I notice where clumps need to be divided or overgrown bushes completely cut down. All these on-site cogitations make for more productive and realistic planning than the kind I otherwise do, nodding over the catalogs in front of the fire in the long evenings.

Pruning in other seasons is a miserable, sweaty, prickly job. You can't see what you're doing because of all the leaves, and as often as not you cut the wrong stem by mistake. And you are so uncomfortable, and there is so much else that urgently needs to be done, that you tend to work sloppily and fast just to get it over with. In the winter, you are in a delightful state of exhilaration (once you get moving) and you can see exactly what's going on; you can grab those pesky brambles and briars before they grab you, and cut them off way down at ground level with no obstruction. (Of course, you can't pull them up by the roots when the ground is frozen—nothing is perfect.) But the most important advantage is just being alone with your garden in its nakedness. If it doesn't look good in its nakedness, I personally don't think it is much of a garden.

Pruning is one of the more immediately creative aspects of gardening. For someone like me, who can't draw a recognizable circle but still has a small frustrated aesthetic impulse tucked deep away, pruning seems excitingly akin to sculpture. Like Michelangelo, I stare at the tree or shrub with my mind's eye, trying to discern the ideal shape within the superfluity, and proceeding ever so slowly in order not to cut off unintentionally something I shouldn't. It goes in stages: first everything that is dead or diseased, then whatever is interfering with human passage or a desired vista or the plant's own health, and finally whatever *can* be pared off to reduce the plant to its sparest and most elegant essence. Each cut is taken back to a natural point of branching so that when the job is done you still have a plant that looks like a plant, not a geometrical figure. As with the garden as a whole, the aim is to achieve a tree or shrub that looks more like itself than it did originally. Of course I seldom achieve this lofty aim, but it is the theoretical inner tune to which I try to dance.

Along about the middle of February I start to see the sprouts of daffodils and crocuses; by April first bulbs are in bloom all over the place and I can't keep myself from starting spring cleanup, although it's probably a bit early. Since I put my garden to bed quite tidy and don't use winter mulches there isn't a whole lot of cleanup to do, mainly clearing out concentrations of leaves that have built up in corners and tucking "heaved" plants back into place. As soon as the ground is dry enough to behave like soil rather than mud, I begin digging planting-holes for whatever new things I've ordered, filling them with compost and letting them sit until the plants arrive (if I wait until the packages have actually come, I tend to skimp the digging job in my haste to get them into the ground). Planting time for annuals and tender perennials is traditionally Memorial Day in this latitude, but most of us jump the gun by a couple of weeks and usually get away with it, though once in a long while there is a frosty night even as late as the Fourth of July.

My main spring chore is digging out the good new compost from the "ready" end of my doughnut and carrying it two pailfuls at a time to whatever areas seem to need it most. I generally sprinkle some bone meal over the place where the compost will go, and then apply it about two inches thick; around one- or two-year-old shrubs I keep a layer four to six inches thick, extending out as far as the reach of the longest branches. This is to encourage their young roots to grow strong and deep, and is a strictly temporary luxury; after the second

139

year, shrubs in my garden are on their own unless the soil under them starts looking actually depleted (pale, powdery, and sunken). Any excess compost goes into the big plastic bins to wait until needed.

Considerably before this chore is finished, the April and May rains and the long days of sunshine have resulted in a perfectly tremendous growth of grass and weeds in all parts of the property, and the early-spring feeling of smug satisfaction in my neat, well-cared-for garden vanishes. From now through August, keeping up with the weeds is the main job, and a challenging one it is. The problem for me, as probably for most people, is that my summer is complicated by visits from friends and relations that prevent me from putting the needs of the garden first. While I would certainly rather have the visits than not, still I tend to forget, every year, how little time I am going to have to keep the outdoors decent, and as a result I am always dismayed when it *isn't* decent.

Usually I do manage to get a first overall weeding done, and paths opened up, before company arrives, and all is well for a week or two. But with many plants growing at the rate of two to six inches a day, and with me often not getting into the garden for a week at a time, things do get considerably out of hand. I don't honestly know of any answer to this if one wants to have a summer garden that is different from a winter garden—that is, a garden with fresh shooting and flowering things—and to take care of it oneself.

What I *try* to do is to take at least a quick businesslike walk around the place every two or three days, with clippers and pail in hand and wearing gloves. On such a walk stray branches that threaten people's eyes and hairdos can be nipped back, paths can be kept at least functionally open, gigantic weeds that are suffocating little delicate treasures can be summarily if not permanently dealt with, things that have gone to seed can either be deadheaded or harvested. Probably even more important, I can see on this walk what really *has* to be done and give it some kind of priority in order to avoid total disaster—I can always find an hour sometime during the week, if I'm sufficiently motivated. Using this system means that the garden remains superficially tidy and reasonably attractive even though it is being neglected. I wish I adhered to it more faithfully.

The rate of growth slows down when the rain stops in June, and even more as the days begin to get shorter toward the end of July. Then the primary need of the garden is for water, and in spite of a vast and complex system of hoses, including two "leaking" hoses that just ooze the water onto the ground rather than spraying it into the air to be mostly evaporated, keeping up with the water supply is about all I can manage in August even though I am so stingy with it.

So after Labor Day, when everybody goes away and the days are starting to cool off, I go outside every morning, get down on my knees, and crawl systematically over the whole property pulling up weeds—first the paths, then the areas around the house, then those most visible from inside the house, and finally the outlying bits like the Wild Garden and the Secret Garden. This takes, usually, all my time right up to Thanksgiving, merging gradually into the brush-clearing and pruning activities of winter.

I don't do any planting in the fall, or any dividing of existing plants, since I've found they don't do nearly as well as when I plant them or divide them in the spring. (I do sometimes, in the course of my weeding, move a nice columbine or baby fern that has sprung up in the path or in the middle of something else, to a community of its own kind or to the Wildflower Border; I'm rather casual about this but the transplantees seem to do all right, probably because I only give this treatment to plants I know to be tough.)

In my good years I make a second go-around with the compost pile in the fall, first using up whatever is still available in the big bins and then seeing how much new compost has matured over the summer. I load it into pails and tote it around to wherever it seems apt to do the most good. This, I like to think, serves as a sort of fall fertilizing and also to a small degree makes up for my not mulching my plants. At least there is a good blanket of compost around the roots of things helping them to withstand the violent temperature fluctuations during the winter months.

When I do get everything tidied up and fed before holiday preparations start keeping me indoors too much, I have a complacent wealthy feeling just as if I had harvested an enormous vegetable garden before the frost. And from then on, I can enjoy myself looking out the windows at odd hours pondering the fine points of the winter pruning to be done without any nagging guilt about what I should have done while the ground was still warm enough to sit on and soft enough to pull roots out of.

The Ages of a Garden

The conception of a garden, like that of Fancy, may be said to take place in the eye when it first rests on a domestic landscape and finds it improvable. After a relatively brief gestation period during which a spade and a hoe are acquired and, it is to be hoped, books or other sources consulted, the newborn gardener (whose age *as* a gardener is identical, of course, with that of his or her creation) breaks the soil and introduces something that was not there before, and lo! a garden exists. It is not much yet but it is, categorically, a garden.

The infant garden and its mentor, the infant gardener, are wrapped up in each other in a state of exclusionary bliss. The garden appears to be the most remarkable one ever planned; its tiniest achievement is hailed as unique and astonishing (my family still teases me about the days when it was shown around the garden "with a magnifying glass" because its wonders were not apparent to the naked eye). No work is too great, no vision of the future too brilliant for inclusion in the besotted gardener's daydreams. And it really does grow apace and show forth new miracles daily, only perhaps not quite as unprecedented as its maker would like to believe.

There ensues a long and on the whole satisfactory period of continuing development, in which the garden approaches ever more closely the picture in the mind's eye of the gardener. This is partly because the gardener is becoming more skillful at translating these pictures into reality, and partly because increasing experience is leading to pictures that are *capable* of becoming reality in the circumstances of this particular garden. The gardener is finding out that the garden is not really totipotential— that is, that it can only become one kind of garden and not all other kinds simultaneously; indeed, that it can become any kind of garden only with the input of a given amount of continuing effort on the part of the gardener. The amount of effort that can willingly be given then becomes a question the gardener has to grapple with, and hard distinctions have to be made between what is possible, within the constraints of reason, and what is the best one can imagine.

Thus the garden and the gardener go on exerting a mutually salutary discipline, each controlling the other's excesses and severely punishing the other's mistakes. By degrees, and with many a wearisome detour (as well as many a radiant but unrepeatable success), they grow together in wisdom and in stature, and the garden looks better and more like a garden year by year.

A stage of what corresponds roughly to adolescent rebellion occurs when, after years of submitting more or less to the gardener's direction, the garden rather abruptly pulls itself together, shakes off the yoke, and declares in unmistakable terms that it is henceforth to be considered autonomous—it will no longer abide by the gardener's misguided ideas for its future. The wise gardener (this is where philosophy comes in), after the first painful gasp, recognizes that the garden is indeed coming into its own and stops trying to force it into the unsuitable molds dictated by his or her own emotional hangups ("But I *always wanted peonies!*"); presently, in fact, there arrives a sense of astonished pride at what the garden turned out to be, after all, in its own right.

There comes a time when the basic plan is all in place and only relatively minor additions and changes need to be made. The garden is now mature; the trees and shrubs that were planted as slender twigs now occupy their full allotted space, the perennials that have survived the sorting-out process of the years are suited to their locations and thriving, the ground covers perform their comfortable work of rounding out the various pictures. The gardener is more relaxed these days; he happily supplies the labor necessary for maintenance, and thoroughly enjoys the ongoing interaction which, if it has lost some of its early excitement, has also stopped breaking his heart quite so regularly. He has learned that what is killed by a hard winter can be replaced; that if one low-growing pink flower doesn't do well in a given location another one will (and the first one may well prosper in a different location); that even the devastation of a hurricane can stimulate a new and better design (or, at the worst, stand as an honorable historic landmark). And he has learned to confine his experimentation to what he is going to be able to take care of through the seasons.

All these steps I have experienced in relation to my own garden, and there was a period when I assumed, unconsciously, that the last stage I have described was the end of the story. When I arrived at this point, I imagined, my garden and I would go hand in hand into the sunset, time would stand still, and nothing else would ever happen. I was quite wrong; biological systems are not like that.

I had, in fact, barely begun to look around the place with some sense of stable achievement when various subtle signs notified me that my years of unrestricted vigor in wrestling with the soil and its products were coming to a close. I became aware of wanting a rubber pad to kneel on even on relatively non-stony ground; of aching and swelling in fingers and wrists after a hard bout of weed pulling; of increasing difficulty in pruning branches that I could have clipped easily a few years before; and of simple physical fatigue after comparatively brief exertion. This is not yet a serious problem; so far I can still put in a good two to three hours at a session; but it used to be five hours at a session, and more than one session in a day. The handwriting is on the wall.

One obvious expedient is to hire someone else to do the work, and I suppose that eventually this is the only recourse. The question is, though, how long can I put off that "eventually"? As long as I can crawl out there, *I* want to be the one who does the trimming and the weeding and the dividing. This work has become part of my identity; I can't bear the thought of my occupation being gone. If I keep the garden healthy, it does the same for me, physically, mentally, and spiritually. Clearly the only resolution to this dilemma is to cut the job down to my size; and clearly this means redesigning the garden to some degree so that an older gardener *can* handle it, at least for an extended further period.

It is a curious fact that, at the same time one's physical limitations become apparent, one's taste tends more and more toward the simple and unpretentious effects that take less maintenance. I really don't know which is the primary factor, the decline of physical energy or the development of a more sophisticated and subtle taste; but it seems I am not alone in moving in this direction as the years go by. I can remember several authors whose books describe the same sequence; and I can remember, too, how mistaken I thought them and how tame their later productions seemed to my then burgeoning imagination. Now I have traveled the same path and you, gentle reader, will probably do so too, in time.

In my case the move toward a simpler planting has itself been a gradual and simple process. In each part of the garden, as things multiply and compete and need to be thinned out, I look critically at what is flourishing best, what seems most at home, what gives the best visual impact for the greatest part of the year. This I divide and allow to spread, while less characteristic or more distracting or "fussy" plants are firmly pulled up or at least confined to a single sharp accent for a particular purpose.

Thus, in the Rock Garden I am replacing most other perennials as they die out with heaths and heathers, to give a more homogeneous, less spotty overall look. The moss pinks are being allowed to spread a little farther year by year. All these grow so solidly that weeds have very little chance with them; a minimal trimming once a year keeps them in shape. Substantial accents like the Japanese spirea and large clumps of alyssum, geranium, and thrift, which give good solid bloom for an extended period and are decorative even when out of bloom, are also still encouraged. But dozens of little treasures whose overall impression is insignificant or even pathetic, but which I have cherished for their very fastidiousness and elusiveness, are no longer getting special treatment but are being allowed to fade out or be overrun, looking forward to the day when the Rock

Garden will have to fend largely for itself but when I will still want something agreeable to look at out of my window.

A similar development is going on in the Wildflower Border, which over a period of several years became a veritable sampler of the most vigorous and invasive wildflowers of the area, my heart rejoicing as my childhood favorites came into bloom each in turn. This border takes a surprising amount of care, because although I hardly feed it at all, it still has to be kept groomed and deadheaded and free of grass, and the most aggressive plants kept from overwhelming all the rest; and many of the fall bloomers look best if they're pinched back once or twice during the summer. All this is a good deal of work, most of it painstaking and detailed, done on the knees along the whole sixty-foot length of the border; it's necessary if the effect I've wanted, that of a blooming border (even a wild one), is to be maintained.

So, while I'm not yet ready to give up the Wildflower Border, I can see that my ability to keep it presentable will eventually decline. In the meantime, the vinca ground cover that I started in this area many years ago has finally established itself as a more or less solid carpet under and amongst everything else; and some year, not too far in the future, when I'm cleaning up in the fall I will simply pull up all the wildflowers and leave the vinca, a thoroughly satisfactory and trouble-free plant.

On the west side of the house the planting, after years of strenuous effort, has settled down to an unadventurous but pleasing mixture that includes the oldest and most reliable of Old Reliables: tulips, columbines, astilbe, daylilies, and hosta. I still play around each year with other things, and fill in the gaps with annuals, but as these eminently satisfactory plants multiply they are taking up more and more of the space, and I can readily foresee the day when this border will maintain itself with almost no help from the (by then decrepit) gardener. I see no reason why it couldn't get along for ten years or so after I have stopped rendering any care at all, still faithfully producing excellent bloom from May to September.

You see the point. While I can't help regretting the necessity of retiring from a more energetic interaction with my garden, it is going to happen whether I like it or not. And without some advance planning, it seems to me that the old age of the garden is going to be characterized by weediness and disorder and a general sense of decay, whereas *with* planning it can remain a place of dignity and refreshment for many years.

I hope to be here to enjoy it.